There Are No Mistakes

There Are No Mistakes

Becoming Comfortable with
Life As It Is, Not As It *Should* Be

Eleanor Wiley
with
Caroline Pincus

CONARI PRESS

First published in 2006 by Conari Press,
an imprint of Red Wheel/Weiser, LLC
York Beach, ME
With offices at:
500 Third Street, Suite 230
San Francisco, CA 94107

ISBN 978-1-57324-262-2

Typeset in Hoefler Text, by Jonathan Sainsbury.

Printed in the U.S.A.

To my three children,

Stewart, Beth Ann, and Jennifer.

They have been my most beloved teachers.

Contents

Acknowledgments

My gratitude to all the people who have supported me as I worked on this book is more than I can express in words. I am so grateful to Jan Johnson for publishing these words and for introducing me to Caroline Pincus. Gratitude to Caroline, who crafted the jumbled words I gave her into the wonderful stories you will read in the pages that follow. I also gained a friend in the process.

I also thank all the other people at Red Wheel Weiser/Conari Press who contributed to the publication of this book, including Pam Suwinski, the eagle-eyed copyeditor.

I am not going to name all of the wonderful people who trusted me with their stories, because then they wouldn't be anonymous, as I promised them they would be. They know who they are, and to them I send my gratitude. A deep bow of gratitude, too, to my walking buddies who listened to me, my family, my spiritual communities who prayed with me, and all the people I have encountered along the way who are part of this book. And last but not least you, because you bought the book! Thank you, one and all.

Introduction

If you were to meet me you would think, *Now there's a woman who is comfortable with life as it is.* I keep my hair short, wear comfortable clothes and shoes, and always adorn myself with some of my art. I smile a lot—and am easily moved to tears—and I am constantly displaying enthusiasm for the simple things around me. In other words, people can tell that I'm enjoying myself.

Suffice to say, this wasn't always the case. For much of my life I worked very hard to make it look as if I had it all together. If I made a mistake I covered it up; if I didn't know the answer I made one up. Until I was in recovery I struggled continually with the question, Am I doing the *right thing?* The truth is, no matter where I was or what I was doing, I never really felt at home, and I was never convinced that I really belonged—anywhere.

That didn't change until I was fifty-four. That was the year I recognized I was an alcoholic and discovered the twelve-step program of Alcoholics Anonymous (AA). I'll never forget walking into an AA meeting for the first time and hearing people say, "I am a grateful alcoholic." I was sure they were out of their minds. I was even more sure that I would never, ever say such a thing. Well, I was wrong. I *am* a grateful alcoholic—grateful, especially, to have been pushed into telling myself the truth about my life, to have been pushed to discover that there are no mistakes in life, only choices, and that beautiful things can come from what we think of as our mistakes. The stories I had the opportunity to finally *hear* through AA forced me to explore and become comfortable with life as it is and to stop making up stories of how I wished it would be. AA didn't force; it gave me an opportunity I was willing to take.

For example, long after my marriage was over I hung on to it, telling myself the story that if I just did one more thing, my husband would come back. I blamed myself for not being good enough to keep him happy, not knowing the right thing to do. It took time and lots of therapy for me to understand that we are each responsible for our own happiness, that what I did was right.

Another story I told myself when my daughter Beth Ann died was that if I just got on with my life, things would be fine. I told myself that strong people can handle these things. Of course that didn't work. The death of a child rocks your whole world, and I needed time to grieve. And with my drinking, I spent years telling myself stories to make believe things were okay. I could always find an excuse for my drinking behavior, for needing to unwind, to relax. That is, until I admitted I was an alcoholic and got into recovery.

At age seventy, I continue uncovering what is right for me; I continue to work at being comfortable with life as it is and to stop struggling with how I wish it would be. And one of the great tools I have discovered along the way has been beads. Yes, you read it right. *Beads.* It might be something else entirely for you, but the catalyst for me was beads, which came into my life about four years after I stopped drinking and was on my way to recovery. Let me explain.

About twelve years ago a friend asked me to help her make some necklaces. I told her I didn't know how. Betty's response was a revelation. "It doesn't make any difference," she said. "I'll show you." What was so remarkable about this for me was that earlier in my life I would never have been able to say, "I don't know how." Allowing myself to do so was a huge step, and it opened up an amazing world for me. The more comfortable I became with not knowing, and acknowledging out loud that I didn't know, the more other people were willing to share their wisdom, to open new doors for me, and to invite me into new places. I also discovered—and continue to discover—how very much I *do* know, simply from being alive and paying attention.

Through surrendering to the process of beading—of choosing the beads and materials and putting them together on a strand—I am offered a way of looking at life without judgment. There is no right or wrong way to string beads, no right or wrong choices. And that's the way it is with life. There are no right or wrong choices; there are only different—and sometimes arduous!—paths to wholeness. That's the lesson in the beads for me. Once we peel off the layers of "supposed to be" we have been hiding behind, once we realize that *there is no one right way,* we are able to see the rocks along our path not as obstacles but as opportunities to climb higher and get a better view. We can see the road ahead.

I have traveled an amazing distance—emotionally, spiritually, and geographically—since I started working with beads. When I started out, my life was in flux. Now I exhibit, teach, and speak about beads all over the world. I have borne witness as hundreds of others have discovered that sometimes the greatest works of beauty come from our "mistakes." I work hard, but I am amazed on a daily basis as I look at the gifts that the beads have placed in front of me.

There are no mistakes.

A few years ago, I was asked to craft a symbol that would be inclusive of all faith traditions for a bead kit project that my agent wanted to shop around to publishers. Using various crafts as spiritual tools was a really hot idea at that time, and my agent thought people would go for a strong interfaith symbol. Being who I am, I said, "Sure, I can do that." In truth, I had no idea what I was doing. Then I remembered a talk about the Sacred Wheel given by one of the original organizers of the Parliament of the World's Religions, Jim Kenny, at the gathering in 1993. By some miracle, I found the tape of his talk and, inspired, drew a mandala that included all spiritual paths. I had the idea that it could be made into a medallion, but because I didn't have the technical skill necessary to carve the wax mold necessary for producing a medallion, I needed to ask for help.

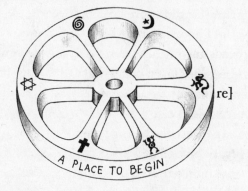

A PLACE TO BEGIN

At the time, my ex-husband Graham, his wife Claudia, and I were working on creating a comfortable family relationship for ourselves and our children and grandchild. Graham has great technical skill, and I asked him if he would carve the wax. This was a big, big step for us. He agreed, and now everyone in our family has this beautiful medallion designed by their mother and created by their father, a true symbol of peace and reconciliation. Such a thing certainly couldn't have happened early in our divorce.

The kit project never happened, but I do sell the medallion -- wherever I go. It obviously speaks to people. Its archetypal symbols represent many faith traditions, and to me it speaks to our inherent wholeness, our inclusive nature, and the fact that it simply doesn't work to deny anyone else's reality—or any one part of our own. That what makes this planet spin is the *all* of it. I have been told by many people that they choose the wheel as a symbol for their life.

I always invite people to attach their own meanings to the symbol. For me, the wheel symbolizes the healing of my relationship with my ex-husband. Believe me, that's no mistake. It truly makes life more comfortable. But when I look at the wheel from the perspective that it also symbolizes my family of origin, I see that it wobbles a bit, representing the mental illness and alcoholism that runs through my family, and the denial we all had about it for so long.

In my travels people often ask me, "How did you get where you are today?" "How do you know if you are doing it *right?*" The fact is, I *don't* know. But I have become comfortable with not knowing. That is what the beads and life have taught me. The amazing, wonderful, and ordinary people who have been willing to share their stories with me have also shown me that each and every one of us can find our path to wholeness if we give ourselves the time and permission to slow down and pay attention, to discover what is right for us as individuals. Through this book I hope to share some of the most important gifts I have received from the gift of listening.

As I travel and talk with so many people who are finding their own ways to wholeness, I often ask them if they would be willing to talk to me about how they got to be where they are. Often they'll say, "Oh, I don't know anything special," or "I don't know enough." The truth is, *we all know enough*. As I was told over and over again in early recovery, just look at your own life. You *do* know.

That, too, was one of my reasons for writing this book. I set out to write it after seven years of teaching, not because I think I know *the* right way, but because I wanted to share some of the wonderful stories people have told me—stories about finding beauty in the midst of our darkness and surprise blessings in our struggles toward wholeness. You must remember that all these stories are filtered through me, and how I understood them might not jive exactly with the way the storyteller intended them to be heard. I hope that I have honored each and every person who trusted me with their story.

As a reader, your "listening" to their stories is a way of bearing witness to their struggles, but it is also my hope that their stories give you permission to tell your own truths—to family, to friends, to yourself. Speaking our truths out loud, we no longer have to be afraid; we're no longer alone; we don't have to carry our life's burdens on our backs. We become joined in community with others who are trying to find their way in this chaotic world.

You will also find here suggestions of things you can do to begin your exploration, as well as Practices to help you become comfortable with life, with *your* life, just as it is. You see, we don't have to fix each other, we don't have to *know* the right way or path, but by bearing witness we tell each other that our lives are alright just the way they are. This is an invitation to you—to trust yourself and your way of walking through the world, to notice your discomfort and shift to comfort. It is an invitation to acceptance.

Several of the people who contributed their stories wished to remain anonymous, so I changed identifying details for everyone. But, as I see it, each and every person I talk about in this book is a part of my community, a part of my family. Let this new family hold your hand and support you as you explore your path. Remember: It is your path, your journey. You know what is right, what is comfortable, what will work for you. Trust yourself. This is a journey without end, but it begins with the willingness to look at your life and see the rocks in your path not as obstacles but as opportunities to climb higher and get a better view. That's what each of the people described in this book found a way to do, and we invite you to get to know them as they are, not as you (or they) might wish them to be.

This family-they are just ordinary people like you and me, stumbling their way toward wholeness. Welcome to their stories of joy and pain, of what has helped them climb over the rocks and boulders they found on their paths, and the peace they have found in the process of becoming comfortable with life as it is.

One final note: You can start this book with chapter 1 and read it from start to finish or just skip around and read the chapters that interest you most. That's entirely up to you. This is your book and your time. I invite you to explore it in whatever way is comfortable for you.

Namaste.

1

Honor Where You Came From

A man I once knew told me he didn't want to go into therapy to find himself because he was afraid he would find nothing there. That kind of sums it up, doesn't it? So many of us live with a profound fear of looking at who we are and how we got to be this way. No matter how often our patterns come back to bite us, we're afraid to look at them. But no one becomes comfortable with life as it is without somehow grappling with the ways they carry around their pasts, either by replicating them or desperately rejecting them, or even — and often — both.

I'm not just talking about the social or economic class we may have come from, or our race or ethnicity or religion, although all of these have certainly played their parts in shaping who we are. I'm talking about the emotional climate within our childhood homes and what we learned about ourselves and the importance (or lack of importance) of our needs and all the little peculiarities of the way we were raised. I'm talking about the family secrets and the shame and all the particular circumstances and people that shaped our personalities. I'm talking about the painful stuff *and* the good stuff.

Laughter may have rung through the hallways of your home, or you may have heard shouting all the time. You may have been encouraged to speak your mind, or you may have learned that that was a terribly dangerous thing to do. You may have a very definite sense of "home"—the place where you lived, perhaps, for your entire childhood, or you may have no idea what it means to feel physically and emotionally at home. The point is, although you did not choose the circumstances of your birth or upbringing and you did not control what tribe or tribes you were born into, those circumstances and conditions made their mark on you and undoubtedly have a profound effect on you still.

Becoming comfortable with life as it is involves honoring where you came from—all of it. Not necessarily liking it, mind you, but coming to seeing how it shaped you, and making adult choices based not in ignorance and denial but in courage and awareness of your past. You see, what happens when we try to ignore the lingering effects our starter kit has on our lives, we end up walking around in a world of illusion. We may think we're not very bright or that we don't matter or that we don't fit in, but it's not true. Once we can let go of those illusions and face how we became who we are, we can develop the capacity to be alright within ourselves, to recognize that no matter where we came from or what happens, we'll be alright.

Let's say you grew up in a climate of financial instability or chaos. If you don't pay attention to how that fear still affects your world-view, you can easily be eaten up by anxiety. And even if you end up having more money than God, you may stay wound up with worry; you may never feel comfortable or able to enjoy your good fortune. By contrast, you may have grown up quite comfortable, with all the trappings, but chose a profession for which the pay isn't all that great. Perhaps you still don't own a home or have any of the other markers of "success." You can fret endlessly about not having the luxuries to which you were accustomed, or you can decide that money isn't the defining factor of life and commit to enjoying your life without the benefits of a big bank account. In order to be a really sound choice, however, the second option requires making peace with what money meant in your childhood and making a conscious choice to shift that meaning *now*. It may take years of ongoing inner work to let go of certain judgments and feelings of shame. But the outcome is that you will *know* that your choice to live differently is a sound one—not just a rejection or rebellion but a choice based in your own adult values.

Tuning In to the Subtle Stuff

The messages we pick up from our starter kits can be subtle or quite overt. I come from a big family and very early on picked up the subconscious message that I was just one big mistake. Although you wouldn't have known that if you'd met me—I always looked like I had it together—I didn't feel like I fit in anywhere. Until pretty recently, in fact, I carried around this sense of not belonging, of being a mistake. It wasn't until my granddaughter asked me one day, "Momo, what was it like to be the youngest of nine children?" that I faced this part of my starter kit dead on. Hearing myself say to her, "It was very lonely and I didn't feel very important," was a revelation to me. I had never seen it quite so clearly before: That really *was* my core feeling about myself all these years: I didn't feel very important at all.

I didn't even realize that was how I was feeling. I just thought I was some kind of a misfit. Coming to terms with myself and my role in my family, for example, has been a lifelong process. But hearing myself articulate these buried feelings to my granddaughter, I could feel how real they still were. I decided I would make a set of prayer beads representing each member of my family and focus on connecting with them in my heart. I then strung all the beads onto a cord, along with the Sacred Wheel of Peace I had created as a meditation tool, and put them in my living room, where I'd see them often.

Since then I have moved the beads around my house and studio, but each time I come upon them I pick them up and say a prayer for each person. It hasn't changed the persons, but it has changed how I feel about them and about me—and that's the best I can do. As I pray over the beads and think about my family of origin, I continue to discover the influence my early life had on what I do and how I feel as an adult.

Discovering Your Core Description

Part of honoring your starter kit has to do with discovering your core description, that genetic and emotional blueprint we get from childhood. No matter what it is, whether you were taught to feel entitled to everything or nothing, your core description is worth looking at, because it is affecting everything you do, and it will bring you low at some point if you don't face it. For example, my core description was alcoholism, at least for many years. It included being the youngest of nine and not very visible or important; it also included a strong sense of justice and loyalty to community and a "You can do anything" ethic. But part of that was also a sense of inadequacy. In every core description there are conflicting messages, and part of getting in touch with that core is about seeing those conflicts and trying to heal the splits within ourselves.

Another aspect of my own starter kit was that I lived in a very, very small universe, a closed realm. Until I was sixteen, I never traveled more than 60 miles from home. I went to a strict Catholic school where you didn't ask questions and the rules were spelled out. I'm still afraid of not following the rules; such was the power of my upbringing. And I felt really lonely.

My friend Jo also felt exquisite loneliness as a child. She was born in Africa, where she was free to roam and explore. A wonderful African man took care of her from the minute she was born. (In Africa it is not unusual to have a male nanny.) She always felt loved and protected by him. She felt safe.

When Jo talks about her childhood, it sounds incredibly exotic to me, but to Jo it was just the way life was—until she was torn away from everything she knew and loved and moved to Australia, where she felt disconnected and was incredibly lonely and homesick.

Part of what drove Jo for years, as it did me, was a search for belonging, a search to overcome a core loneliness that had stayed with her well into adulthood. Recognizing that our profound sense of isolation and loneliness comes from early childhood has been very liberating for Jo and for me. We still feel the loneliness sometimes, but now we can bring ourselves out of it more readily. And that's really what becoming comfortable with life as it is is all about. We can't go back and change those forces that shaped us, but we can choose how to go forward *with* them.

Jack's starter kit was very different. From the time he was born he was expected to get a sports scholarship to his father's alma mater. That was just the way it was going to be, and Jack knew it. And he worked hard at it, too. He did indeed get that scholarship and was playing by the family rules—that is, until the day he dove into a swimming pool and injured his spine. Good-bye sports, good-bye scholarship, good-bye identity.

Jack took a long detour into alcohol and pain pill addiction before he was able to become comfortable with his life. And he couldn't become comfortable until he gave up the image of life that came with his starter kit. He could never have imagined doing anything "less than" becoming a successful sports figure and had no idea who else he could be. It took a lot of work before he realized that there are other valid choices. He had to become comfortable with his disability and realize that he could develop other talents. Once he did so, he discovered a passion for writing, and now he is a wonderful teacher and writer. This certainly wasn't in the family script. And even in his writing life he is not the BIG man his family had always imagined. But now he knows that the size of the man (or woman) isn't necessarily measured by how well you follow the script. Sometimes you have to throw out the script and start over, but you have to *know* the script first to ensure that you're not just blindly following along.

No matter what class or race or background you might come from, you bring with you values and attitudes and expectations that have been in some sense defining you all your life. And when you honor where you came from, things just aren't as scary. You no longer have to carry the heavy baggage of the past or be as haunted by family demons.

On the physical level, you might discover that you have a family history of diabetes. Knowing this, you can take preventative steps or seek help and make wise choices. Choosing to ignore your starter kit, on the other hand, could land you in the hospital, completely unprepared.

On the emotional level, you might look back and see if there's a family history of anxiety or depression or bipolar disorder. Whether you subscribe to the view that we are our genes or are molded largely by environment doesn't matter. What matters is that being aware of a family pattern of mental or emotional disturbance prepares you to watch for signs, to become informed, and to be less afraid if you end up inheriting the family trait. Remaining ignorant of your starter kit won't help you. Honoring your roots, by contrast, enables you to make choices and helps you develop a capacity for resilience that will be useful for the rest of your life.

Beyond the physical and emotional, there is also the level of spirit. Some of us were taught to question and stay curious about life and meaning; but many, like me, were inculcated from very early on, both in church and at home, that everything has an answer. We weren't allowed to question. Life had its right and wrong, good and bad, black and white. Many of us who had to follow those rigid rules and learned that all the answers come from on high have had a great deal of difficulty learning to trust our own insights and instincts and answers.

Not that the Catholic Church was all bad—not by a long shot. It was from the church (and, by extension, my very Catholic mother) that I learned great respect for mystery and a strong sense of service and gratitude to others. My interest in justice, my desire to be generous and giving—all these flow directly from my Catholic upbringing. But learning to trust my own mind and heart took years.

Honoring your roots, by the way, has nothing to do with shifting blame or placing responsibility for your difficult life onto the people who "made you that way." You are responsible for your own actions. But how much better it is to accept that responsibility with your eyes wide open. Honoring your roots simply means working *with* what you've been given and not feeling so utterly responsible for every choice you make and word you utter. It means recognizing that all of us are a gorgeous mix of inheritance and intention.

Practice: Remembering Your Starter Kit

Find an old picture of yourself, preferably from your early childhood. Sit with the picture for a few quiet moments and see what feelings and memories surface. Look into your childhood face and see what you find there. What do you remember about yourself as a little girl or boy? What do you remember about "home"? What was the defining emotional current? Were your parents always tense or stern? Did they worry a lot? Was there enough money, as far as you know? Was one or both of your parents a drinker? A depressive? Was there a lot of screaming at home? Did you have a lot of fun? Did you laugh a lot as a family, even when things were hard? Did you feel safe?

Think about how the emotional climate within your childhood home still defines you and what things you could begin to do to honor that old skin but move on.

Take the time to explore your physical, emotional, and spiritual roots. Be aware of what has stayed with you; think about what you learned about being human in your earliest childhood. Keep an attitude of openness and curiosity about your past. That's all you can ask of yourself—and it's plenty.

Approaching your life as an archaeologist would, you will experience the excitement, if not always the great joy, of discovery. You may discover that even after all those years of rebelling you are *still* just like your mother. But isn't it better to know that, and then choose how to deal with it, than to just become more and more like her each day, but oblivious or resentful?

When we honor where we come, we discover that we are neither wholly independent of our roots, nor do we have to be controlled or constrained by them. We have many choices about how to live. And we simply can't become comfortable with life until we make peace with how we got here.

2

Own Your Own Pain, Hurt, and Vulnerability

Our culture puts so much pressure on us to be tough and strong. It's considered bad taste to admit to feeling pain, and it often feels like there's no room at all for doubts, for feeling hurt and vulnerable. But every life has its share of pain, and people who are comfortable with life as it is know how important it is to be open and honest about their limits and about what hurts or makes them afraid—in effect, to own their pain.

How do we find the right balance? What do we do when we're not quite up to the task or feel vulnerable? How do we know when to push ourselves and when to go easy? How do we admit that we can't do everything?

You know that old saying, "No pain, no gain"? Well, I'm not convinced about that. Yes, we all have to learn to accommodate some pain and discomfort into our lives, but we also need to mind the difference between accepting our pain and inflicting pain on ourselves by ignoring discomfort and pushing ourselves past our own limits.

I am sure you have watched people destroy their knees because, in the name of cardio fitness, they ignored the pain that came from running on hard surfaces in the wrong shoes, or from forcing their legs into the Lotus position for meditation in the name of spirituality. It's so easy to get caught up in striving for a goal and forgetting that we are whole people, with bodies, minds, and spirits that need to be cared for equally.

A friend of mine was watching a gymnastics meet recently and observed a twelve-year-old girl competing while she had the flu. The child had apparently thrown up all the way to the gym. Now she was doing her routine and then heading for the bathroom and throwing up, and then returning for the next exercise. What was this young girl learning about pain? Where do we draw the line between owning and ignoring pain and discomfort?

It's a matter of balance. People who are filled with pain, hurt, and vulnerability simply can't move forward in life. Everything scares them to death. They have to find appropriate outlets for talking about their pain. They have to learn to reach out and ask for help without wallowing or becoming too self-obsessed. But when we push ourselves beyond our limits or are unwilling to acknowledge our limitations, we can't expect others to honor our limitations either.

Asking for Help

Asking for help when we are in pain is very difficult for many people, so we don't do it. But we often expect others to read our minds and know what we need. Recently I was having a conversation with a group of women who had all had hip replacements, and we got to laughing about what we are able to ask for and what we expected others to imagine we need—and God help them if they imagine the wrong thing! Then the discussion turned to the problem: the need to "pay back." If we accept others' help when we are in need, are we going to be able to pay them back? Does always having to balance the scale prevent us from accepting help? What have we created in our wish for independence, our need to keep things balanced?

Do you think the pioneers thought about payback when they helped each other build houses and barns? Everyone needed help (and we still do), so it just came naturally. Today we have put ourselves into many little isolated boxes, houses, cars, and cubicles, and it is difficult to find our way out into an open space. Working in the hospital as a therapist and an administrator for as many years as I did, I know that the people who could ask for help and graciously accept it were the ones the staff most liked to take care of. Owning our vulnerability and pain makes us all more human. It creates space for others to help us as well as to own *their* vulnerability. It's not such a bad place to be.

Some of us learned early on in our lives to sit with a great deal of discomfort, to the point of putting ourselves at risk, and now we just do it "naturally." What's more, by the time we get around to admitting to being in pain or asking for help, other people have become accustomed to our façade and our superhuman act and often either don't believe us or won't help. They know what we can pull off and they expect us to continue to bear up. When we give people false expectations, we can't be annoyed when they refuse us help.

Sometimes, however, owning our pain puts us in direct conflict with other people. Say you've always done odd jobs for an ill friend, but now you've developed some back problems. Owning your pain and telling your friend that you can no longer help with jobs that require lifting might disappoint or even piss off your friend. She may get resentful or angry or think you're just making excuses; on the other hand she might just treat you to a massage as a thank you for all the help you have been. Of course, you have to weigh the potential fallout of your friend's response against the consequences to your own health of continuing to do the heavy lifting, but your needs matter, too. That's what I've learned from people who are comfortable with their lives as they are.

Gloria had a bone infection and extensive surgery as a child that left her with paralysis in her right leg. It caused her to limp and gave her some chronic pain, and she had to wear a built-up shoe. She could never run as fast as her friends; she could never win a race. For years she acted like she didn't care and kept her pain hidden away, until one day when she was about forty-five. It was as if the storm clouds just blew away and the sun came out. She finally allowed herself to think about how much she had always longed to win a race and acknowledged that the reason she was so competitive at bridge was connected to never having been able to win a race while running. Perhaps most striking of all was the realization that it was okay to admit it!

Gloria's friends knew that her life had to be a struggle, but they were not comfortable asking questions or offering help; the door on that subject had been tightly closed for years. Slowly, slowly, Gloria allowed the door to open. She needed to feel safe and didn't know how she'd react to allowing these feelings to surface. Gloria found a therapist who helped her start the process. Now life is unfolding, and Gloria's family and friends are allowed to see the vulnerable and the capable Gloria. It is a beautiful sight indeed.

Suffering is probably the last thing we want to have to accept and incorporate into our lives, but there it is. Life is not an advertising slogan—all moon, spoon, and June. It's often very, very hard, and sometimes we have to get kicked in the butt repeatedly before we get the message.

I'll never forget one of the kids in my first recovery group almost walking out when I mentioned that I'd had to experience the same pain over and over before I figured out how to make different decisions. Poor guy was under the misguided impression that once we see the light, that's it, and we can move on to something else. Well, that's certainly not how it worked for me or for most of the people I know. Fortunately for him, he had the guts to stay and listen.

When my friend Arlene was diagnosed with cancer, her greatest fear was of dying in pain. She had watched her husband suffer greatly two years earlier and didn't want to go the way he had. Arlene hated doctors; she had not been to see one for thirty-five years. I asked why and she said, "All they do is tell you you're sick." We both laughed at that one.

She did all the treatments and surgery her doctor suggested and finally came to trust her oncologist, but she was afraid to talk with him about her fear of dying a painful death. She just assumed that was the way it sometimes had to be, because that was the way it had been for her husband.

Finally I was able to help her gain the courage to speak with her physician. I listened as she spoke her fears aloud. I believed that her doctor would help her, that no one in this day and age needs to die in pain. When Arlene finally did talk to her doctor about her fears, he assured her that she would have the proper medication to alleviate her pain when the time came. Three days later, Arlene died peacefully in her sleep, with no pain.

Owning our pain, whether it be physical or emotional, gives us the opportunity to minimize our suffering. That's the irony. Pain is inevitable; suffering is not.

Practice: How Well Do You Accept Help?

Devote a day to noticing how many times you refuse help—from help carrying heavy files to help looking after your kids to help with the dishes to help with a project at work. Just notice. If you'd like, get a little notebook and jot down a quick note every time you refuse help. Just a couple of words.

At the end of the day, set aside ten minutes and take an honest look at these episodes from your day. Think about what prevented you from saying "Yes." Did you think you could do it better on your own, whatever "it" was? Would it have taken too much time or been too much trouble to explain what you needed? Were you afraid other people would think you couldn't do your job? Or that you'd have to pay back the favor?

Take a few more days for noticing, if you'd like, until you find yourself noticing right away and muttering, "There I go again, refusing help."

After you get comfortable with noticing what you do and why comes the tough part: saying "Yes." "Yes, I could use some help." Bear in mind that no one expects you to say "Yes" all the time. Just see how it feels to accept help.

Okay, I'm in Charge, Ready or Not

Years ago I facilitated a discussion group in a nursing home. The subject was pain. Joe indicated he wanted to speak. Joe had ALS (Lou Gehrig's disease), and his voice was very quiet. We all paid close attention in order to hear Joe's words, which have stayed with me to this day. "You know," he said, "you can not judge another man's pain. One man might cut his finger with a knife and be in great pain while another man might cut his finger off and not be bothered at all. A man's pain is his own. No one else can be the judge."

Joe was really talking about suffering here. We can't always control the pain, but we are often in charge of our own suffering. And it's only by owning our pain, our hurt, our vulnerability that we can begin to make peace with suffering.

Of course *how* we own our pain and vulnerability usually determines how others view it. One can become vulnerable with grace or become a whining pain in the rear. When we are graceful about our needs, we stand a much better chance of getting them met! It's usually when we can't be clear about our own pain or vulnerability, and we become obnoxious to the people who are helping us, that we become isolated. And, ironically, that's the greatest vulnerability of all.

Sitting in a beading circle one day, a group of us got on the subject of death. No, it was not a morbid conversation, just a conversation. The woman sitting next to me mentioned that she had become a widow at the age of twenty-eight. Her husband had died of cancer right around the same time my daughter died, back in the 1960s, before there was hospice or bereavement groups. Chatting together now, we were able to talk about our pain and vulnerability and about how terrible it had been to have no place to turn. We talked about how grateful we were when Elisabeth Kübler-Ross came on the scene and how our lives today are enriched because we are able to share our experiences with others.

It's our stubborn refusal to admit that we're hurt or vulnerable that causes us more pain and separates us from the world. We can't afford to just walk away from situations because they're too painful; that just hurts us more in the long run. We have to be willing to admit to being vulnerable and hurt; that not only gives others the opportunity to help us but also gives us a chance at healing and resolving.

Believe it or not, it can be a gift to others to allow them to help you. People are willing; they often even crave to give their best attention and care to those who can accept help with grace.

Try it. Admit to your pain, hurt, and vulnerability, even in small ways. Let others help you, and accept their help with grace. Commit to accepting pain but reducing suffering. Most of the time, that's all we can ask of ourselves.

Have you ever tried telling the truth to the grocery checker who asks you how you are? It's kind of amazing what happens. You usually get back an honest response! It's not moaning and complaining to say, "I'm tired," instead of "Fine." It's making connection. The same goes for letting your officemates know when you had a rough night's sleep and might be a little snappy. Then, when you are (snappy), they'll know it's nothing they did; it's just where you are. It does no one any good to pretend you're alright when you're not.

Other people can't read our minds, and we can't expect or receive support if the people around us don't know what's going on with us. But we do have to acknowledge to ourselves and own what is going on inside us before we can explain it to others. Far from being the sign of weakness we usually think it is, admitting to pain, hurt, or vulnerability takes courage. It takes real self-love to be present with what is, but the rewards of honest, authentic connection are absolutely worth the effort.

3

Accept Yourself

Every day we are bombarded with advice and input about how we ought to be, act, look; what we need to do to stay young, sexy; what cars we ought to drive or clothes we ought to wear to show how successful we are. It starts practically before we have language. From the get-go we are rewarded for "gender appropriate" behaviors and censured for inappropriate ones, often suffering hugely on the inside if we don't "fit" the mold. We're teased for being different; we're taught to strive after an image that may be darn near impossible to achieve. We learn very early how important it is to conform.

But what if we choose not to conform—or never could? What happens when we decide that we're tired of carefully cultivating the image other people know as *us?* What happens when we decide to accept ourselves as we are? We take a risk. We risk rejection from the people who claim to love us. We risk losing our way for a while as we stop leaning on all the supports that have been propping up the image. But ultimately that's a price well worth paying. You can't live an authentic life until you begin to question and shed any illusions you may be harboring or projecting about who you are. If nothing else, you deserve better.

Sometimes it's about accepting our own qualities. If you are an introvert, you probably have felt pressure to be more "social" or "friendly." If you are an extrovert, you may have been told you're too loud. But the fact is we are all wired differently. It's okay to be different, to be shy or quiet or to take a few extra moments to respond to a request or suggestion. We'd all do well to accept whatever it is we need to do to take care of ourselves in the world. We come in every conceivable flavor, you know. You may be someone who hates parties or large group gatherings, even though you regularly do a lot of public speaking and love it. These are not the same thing. We might learn better by listening than by reading a book. The point is, we are entitled to know our own limits and preferences and honor them. That's how we make peace with ourselves and the world—by honoring our differences and not by judging each other or trying to conform to standards that simply don't fit who we are.

It might feel easier to conform, even if it brings up feelings of shame and inadequacy rather than give ourselves permission to be different. The problems with playing that game are that we can end up constantly worrying about getting caught as a fake and often feeling uncomfortable in our own skin. It's a good idea to take a look at what makes us uncomfortable in a given situation, but we have to allow for the fact that it may just come down to a matter of personal preference or temperament, and that's okay. We're allowed to be different, allowed to be individuals. We're allowed to honor just exactly who we are, with all the similarities and differences we possess.

I know, for example, that after teaching a full-day workshop, I'm usually pretty wiped out. I may be charged up by the energy of the group, but I just need to be by myself and rest. I don't want to talk to anyone. It took me years to realize that that was simply my preference, and I was entitled to say "No" to invitations to share a meal or stay overnight. In the past I would have felt obligated to accept and then be social with my hostess. That's just the way I was raised. But now

I am able to refuse, explaining that it's nothing personal, but that I like to be alone after teaching all day. It's what I need to stay balanced, and there's absolutely nothing wrong with it.

What Goes Around . . .

I've also found again and again that you get back what you put out. If you're real with other people, they'll tend to be real with you, too. Self-acceptance creates an atmosphere of give and take, where if you need something, others are usually more than happy to help, and vice versa. I know that my own process of self-acceptance really got a jump start when I started meditating. Meditation allowed me to shine a light on myself and see how I was hiding from the world. It allowed me to see how much I was hurting from making believe I was someone I wasn't. And then, as I allowed myself to just be me, without the b-s, I was finally able to stop drinking.

Isn't Acceptance Another Way of Saying "I Give Up"?

Some people think of accepting as giving up, but I believe it is a form of great courage. It means changing your expectations and allowing life to be as it is. (We talk more about the difference between surrender and giving up in chapter 11.)

For many years I worked with old people as a speech pathologist and hospital administrator, and one of the many blessings of that work was that it gave me the opportunity to enjoy and respect (and accept) the process of aging. I'm not trying to pretend it's always easy or pretty to experience the changes in how we look and feel that happen as we age, but if we're very lucky, age is going to catch up with us *all* sometime. As I got comfortable with this idea, I started saying to friends and acquaintances, in a matter-of-fact sort of way, "I am getting old." Almost to a person, they would jump in to reassure me, "Oh, no you're not!" As if that's what I wanted. The plain truth is, Yes, I am aging, and saying it out loud helps me to accept it. If I can't accept the fact of my aging and be prepared for it, I'll just be miserable as my body continues to undergo change. I don't want to be a miserable old person, and I don't want people to be afraid of my age. I want to be present with age and all that age brings with it. That's what becoming comfortable with life as it is is all about. No matter how many facelifts and dye jobs we have, it doesn't change the fact that we're all getting older. In fact, the way I see it, all these efforts to keep ourselves "looking young" often mask not just the truth but our own discomfort with the truth.

When discomfort arises or I find myself unable to accept change, I am ever grateful for the Serenity Prayer ("God, grant me the serenity to accept the things I cannot change, the courage to change the things I can, and the wisdom to know the difference"). During the process of accepting my alcoholism I made myself say it many times a day, whether I needed it or not! Of course, mostly I needed it.

These days I'm not big on God-talk (I'm more comfortable with a more open spirituality), so here's how I say it now:

> *Grant me the serenity to accept the things I cannot change*
> *Change the things I can*
> *And the courage to know the difference.*

I can already see that getting old is going to require me to use that prayer on a regular basis. One of the harder things for me to accept about aging is how it slows me down. I was always a very high-energy person. Now, when fatigue rears its ugly head, I take some time and reflect on the Serenity Prayer and decide my next move. In the past I might have pushed myself to keep going. Now I might very well take a nap! That's about acceptance, too.

Working with old people for as long as I did also let me come to an understanding that being comfortable with life has nothing to do with the soundness of mind or body; it's all tied up in the spirit.

One of the most striking characteristics of people who are comfortable with life as it is is that they seem to have made peace with the fact that one of the only constants in life is change. They have developed a capacity to remain flexible and resilient, to move with grace from one financial or geographical or relationship or employment situation to another. Resilience is one of those wonderful qualities that can actually be taught—and it is usually learned through the school of hard knocks.

Often it takes the skills of many people to help in the process of accepting transitions from one way of being to another. I'm thinking of my friend Gail, who was hit by a drunk driver and permanently injured about twenty years ago. She had been a yoga instructor and had always been incredibly fit. In that blink of an eye, her life changed course. Someone with lesser courage and persistence might have given up and just closed the curtains on her yoga practice. Not our Gail. She had the guts to accept the limitation her injury placed on her, but she never accepted a lesser life. And she never gave up her yoga practice. Yes, she has had to modify many of the poses she does, but as a result she has also gained a far deeper understanding of the spiritual aspect of the practice.

Gail did not do this alone. She worked with a wonderful rehabilitation team, therapists who encouraged her to see life as it is, medication to ease the physical pain, an ever-deepening connection to the Divine, a wonderful family, and her friends. She still maintains the highest level of mobility and now teaches yoga teachers in training. She helps her teachers-in-training understand and explore the spiritual aspects of yoga, that it is far more than an exercise in flexibility. They also come to discover the ethical and moral issues involved in being a teacher. If she had been unable to accept her situation, she might have ended up a bitter person with a very small life.

As in Gail's story, acceptance often involves dealing with some type of loss—of physical ability or a person or a dream. This is a process that can't be rushed; we can't skip steps. Part of dealing with loss involves grief and letting go. We have to give ourselves the time we need to do those things.

When my daughter Beth died, back in the 1960s, everyone told me to get on with my life. I put on a façade and made it look like everything was just fine. I'll never forget the first time other people's stories emboldened me and gave me the courage to look at the reality of my own story. It was 1972, and Dr. Elisabeth Kübler-Ross was giving one of her weekend workshops on death and dying at our local college. This was a subject I had become all too familiar with. When Beth died in 1966, I had no place to go with my feelings, no place where I could talk about my life or anything to do with Beth's death. I lived in the lonely world of a grieving parent wrapped in a fake smile.

The rest of my world wanted me to get back to normal, get on with my life. But at that workshop, for the first time, I saw and heard people who appeared to be okay using the word *dead*. They were able to laugh and cry about the short lives of their children. Here, no one was saying, "Get on with your life." Here, we all knew: This *was* our lives.

Fortunately, today grieving parents—and persons who are experiencing other kinds of grief—can more easily find support in sharing their stories. And they're far less likely to be told to just get on with life. People dealing with loss still suffer the same great pain—only time will ease the pain, and they will always be left with the scars—but they do not have to keep the pain buried. You tell your story, sometimes to complete strangers. They are not there to fix you; they are there simply to witness your story and offer theirs in return.

When I put Beth to bed on the night of February 21, 1966, she was fine. Oh yes, she had a slight case of asthma and her ear was infected, but I was used to that. My kids all suffered from asthma. I had taken her to see the doctor that afternoon and everything seemed fine. I had given her her medicine, and her infection seemed to be clearing up. When I put her to bed, she was happy and acting perfectly normal. When I checked in on her around midnight, her temperature seemed to have broken and she was sleeping peacefully, and when I got back into bed I told my husband not to worry. Then, around 4:00 a.m., something woke him and he went to check on her again. This time she wasn't breathing. The emergency team arrived and she was pronounced dead.

Needless to say, I was devastated, my husband was beside himself, and my other children were confused and bewildered. Her pediatrician was also terribly distraught. Right around the time she died, he had awakened with a nightmare about her, and he wondered if he had missed something

Everyone in my family had to find his or her own way to acceptance. What helped me along that path was meeting with people who had suffered the same pain; people who understood that the hole never goes away; people who are willing to explore the hole, get to know it intimately, figure out how to learn about the hole and what it contains and not be swallowed up by it. Acceptance was like a bequest left to me by my young daughter. The realization of how losing her was going to affect the rest of my life came slowly, bit by bit. Her death taught me that we truly do have only this moment, and that this need not be depressing or scary.

The acceptance that we have only this moment can be profoundly liberating. Each moment is precious; there are no mistakes. Yes, there are moments we wish we had never experienced, but all we get are the moments as they come along. It's up to us how to respond to them, whether to be comfortable with life as it is or not.

It was through accepting the reality of my daughter's death that I also learned that things change. As time passed, I learned to smile again. I learned to see my other two children in a new light, to cherish them and accept them just the way they are. Here is where that good old Serenity Prayer comes into play again—figuring out what we can change and when the only thing we can do is accept. You could say I have gone kicking and screaming into acceptance—and it was one of the best things I ever had to do.

Accepting Our Feelings—All of Them

Back when I was married, my husband used to say to me, "You are such an angry person." For the longest time I would yell back, at the top of my lungs, "No, I'm not!"

Well the fact is, Yes, I was, but it took a long time and sobriety for me to see and accept that anger was part of who I was. As long as I was busy yelling, "No, I'm not!" the anger just loomed, covering up the pain of feeling like no one ever listened to me. But once I accepted the angry, scared part of me, I could do something to change it. Now I can look back at that old me who couldn't accept her anger and laugh. Of course, I also cry a little. Coming to acceptance is sometimes very hard work.

My son also had to work hard at self-acceptance. For years he struggled with dyslexia. School was never any fun for him. It was not until he was able, as an adult, to go to the community college near his home and ask for help that things turned around. Learning became an adventure. He was able to ask for the help he needed and accept the limitations his dyslexia placed on him. Although he'd always thought it would never happen, he was able, with accommodation, to pursue a college education. He still doesn't read for pleasure, but now he listens with great joy.

Celebrating Diversity

I have known many people who have relocated to the United States from other countries, and those who seem to do best are the ones who have managed to become (or stay) comfortable with their "otherness." They enjoy sharing the celebrations of their home country, (i.e., breaking the piñata, baking a special cake from home, etc.) with their neighbors, and don't feel the need to blend in to the woodwork. It's a balancing act, of course. People who try to stay within communities of other immigrants from their home countries often find the transition very difficult. They stay forever outsiders.

On the flip side, we've all seen what happens when people assimilate to the point of forgetting their roots. Everybody loses the richness of diversity. We need the balance. But those who can accept their otherness often find it easier to accept the help that's out there and necessary in order to integrate into a new community. Finding language classes, seeking out the scholarship support that would enable you to go to school, looking for housing help—none of this is possible until you accept where you are.

There are other aspects to this kind of acceptance, too. Having the experience of being treated as "other," and dealing with it, increases our capacity to spot prejudice when it is being practiced against others. In other words, practicing self-acceptance has ripple effects, increasing our compassion for everyone and anyone who doesn't "fit."

Accepting That You've Made a Wrong Choice

Talk about making the wrong choice! Years ago my friend Ginny was a counselor at a Girl Scout camp. She was supposed to take a group of girls and their leader to the top of a mountain and lead them down and back to their camp at the bottom of the mountain. Ginny had been there before and thought she knew where she was going. She thought she knew a shortcut back to the camp. The day came, and the group was dropped off at a campsite at the top of the mountain. "But the truth was I hadn't been there for a year," Ginny said,

> and things had changed. I started to follow the path down
> the mountain. It was clearly marked, but all of a sudden

everything was ripped up. Bulldozers had come in during the winter to gather trees and had totally destroyed the path.

I walked through the rubble trying to pick up the path on the other side of the destruction, but it was nowhere to be found. The terrain became steep and the girls were having a really hard time, tripping and stumbling a lot. I sat confused for a while, then decided we needed to go back to the top of the mountain, where I knew there was a paved road. Unfortunately the road took the long way around but I thought at least I might find someone driving by and get help. Anyway, it was the only way the girls would get home safely.

By this time we were all hot, tired, and thirsty, but we made our way back up the steep mountain. I left the girls in the campground where we had started the day and set off down the paved road to find help. I was frightened, but of course I had to keep going. Those kids were waiting to be rescued.

I kept thinking to myself, "I've never been responsible for so many people in my life. It has to turn out okay."

It was beautiful and quiet on the top of the mountain. Birds circled overhead, crickets buzzed in the tall grasses at the side of the road. Of course I couldn't really enjoy the scenery; I was too scared. I just kept walking down the middle of the road. It's weird, but I kept thinking I heard a car. I'm sure I prayed, but I don't remember that either.

Finally I did hear a car—a truck, actually. It was two hunters. They stopped and asked what I was doing out in the middle of nowhere. I could smell that they'd been drinking; they had guns; I was terrified. What to do?

I told myself to trust that I would be okay, climbed into the truck, and told them where I needed to go. I'm sure I was shaking but they didn't seem to notice. They just took me right to the place I needed to be—the camp at the base of the mountain. I jumped out, said 'Thank you,' and off they went. The head of the camp took me back up the mountain to pick up the girls, and everything worked out after all.

Many wrong choices were made that day. Now that some time has passed, Ginny and I are able to reflect on all the metaphors for our journeys through life that are held in that one simple story. Falling and stumbling down the mountain (like the girls), thinking we know what we are doing (like the leader), climbing back up the mountain, fear and terror at the rescue. And on and on it goes. What we realized is that getting lost is often a gift. It might not feel like a gift at the time, and it demands a great leap of faith. But it offers us a chance to discover our own strengths, learn from our intuition. It jolts us awake and it calls on us to accept ourselves as we are.

Accepting That We Don't Have to— and Often Can't—Do It All

One of the ways people seem to avoid looking at their lives and accepting what is is by overdoing. I may sound old-fashioned, but I find it hard to watch young people striving to do it all and have it all. Everyone seems to be working too much so they can have more things, and the word *stress* pops up in conversation far too often. For many people, being comfortable and enjoying life seems to be out of reach.

When I was visiting Tucson last winter, I met a woman named Lynn. She was getting ready to move. She hesitantly explained that she and her husband were getting a smaller house, and she wondered if they were going backward. Lynn had a high-powered job that she liked, but now that she had two small children it had become crazy. She and her husband had come to realize that there was simply no time to do all the things that needed doing, and they were missing out on too much of family life. Everyone seemed to be on a merry-go-round. Lynn longed to be a stay-at-home mom, to experience the firsts in her kids' young lives.

Lynn's job had the best benefits, but her husband's paid the most. Lynn plucked up her courage, asked her company about a change, and learned that she could cut back to half-time and retain her benefits (the company really needed her skills). This would give her the time she wanted to be with her children, but she and her husband would no longer be able to afford the payments on the big house. And so, choices were made.

Yes, it takes courage to take a step back and *choose* to give up what is touted as the American Dream, but think of the rewards for Lynn's whole family. Having time to breathe, they realized, was probably more important than the lovely home and the three-car garage.

I don't remember if it was from a movie or a book, but I remember the phrase, "Stop the world, I want to get off." I cheer on the young people who are trying to do things differently, who are stepping off the do-it-all, have-it-all Tilt-a-Whirl and taking the time to enjoy their lives and be with their families. There's nothing wrong with strolling through life one event at a time, with rest stops in between. That's what becoming comfortable with life as it is is all about.

Practice: I'm Okay

For this practice, notice how you respond to compliments and try just saying, "thank you" without excuses. If someone tells you you have on a pretty dress, you really don't have to say, "Oh, that old thing!" or "This? I got it at the Salvation Army!" Just say, "thank you" and see how that feels. If someone tells you you are doing a good job, just say thank you and let that be that. Notice the change that takes place, whatever it is. Just notice.

Accepting the Good Stuff, Too

Just as hard—and just as necessary—as it can be to accept our limitations is to learn to accept the good and wonderful things in our lives.

I earn my living making and selling contemporary prayer beads and giving workshops about stringing beads as a form of prayer. But I didn't start stringing beads until I was in my fifties. When I started out I never thought of myself as an artist. I had no formal training, no art background; I was just doing something that I liked to do. In fact it was years before I could call myself an artist. I figured I hadn't suffered enough or toiled enough or studied enough to qualify. If it comes naturally, it's not a "real" talent. Right?

Wrong. Part of self-acceptance is about honoring what comes naturally to us and accepting the gift.

I know an artist named Clyde who started doodling, making beautiful little pictures, when he was just a teenager. His talent for figurative art was quite amazing. He could carve the most intricate little sculptures, but he never could accept that what he did was really good. He never explored what he might do with this talent because he never could accept that he had it. Any time someone would tell him how good a piece was, he would quickly point out the mistakes he felt were the most prominent part of the piece. It is only now, now that he has retired, that he is coming to an acceptance of his talent and can enjoy his work and not just see its flaws.

Another friend, Mary Jane, has amazing academic skills. She works hard, and she can learn anything she sets her mind upon. But when you try to praise her for it, she'll argue and resist. What is it about acknowledging our strengths that is so damn hard? Is it a fear of other people's envy? Is it just years of training in good manners or not want-ing to brag? We certainly make our lives less comfortable when we can't accept our own strengths and talents.

Acceptance is about *all* of who we are—our strengths, our doubts, the truth of where we come from and how it shaped us—all of it.

4

Tell Your Story—and Allow It to Evolve

Once you get into the habit of practicing self-acceptance, it becomes more and more possible—and important—to share your story. The more we share our stories, our perspectives, and what's true for us, the less alone we feel, the less crazy or different or out there—in other words, the more self-accepting. Of course, we need to choose our opportunities carefully. Not everyone wants to hear about *you* all the time. And most of us need to feel safe before speaking out; we need to know that someone will be listening before we put our stories out there. But being able to say out loud, "I have chronic pain," or "I am a sober alcoholic," or "I am gay," or "I was always told I should be an accountant because I'm good with numbers, and I tried it for a while and made good money, but now I'm going to go to social work school because my passion is to work as an advocate for battered women." Telling our stories honors and validates the tough roads we've all walked; hearing each other's stories broadens everyone's sense of what is possible.

One of the marvelous things about telling our stories to each other is that we often discover missing pieces along the way. We find ourselves saying things we'd never even *thought* before—truths that we hadn't known until we started talking.

Granted, the whole business of sharing our stories is a hard one for many of us, especially those of us who were trained early and often to honor privacy. But not being open and truthful about who we are can cause us great and unnecessary pain. My friend Joan was one of the last people who contracted polio before the vaccine was discovered, and she was left with substantial disabilities. Married and with a couple of small kids, she was determined to carry on a "normal" life. She vowed the polio would never keep her down. She was only in her early twenties and had no road map on how to proceed, so she buried her fears and got on with the work of recovery. For years, she rarely, if ever, talked about her polio.

In spite of what turned out to be permanent limitations, Joan went on to accomplish more than the average person might do in a lifetime. She had several more children, even though her doctors thought that it was a bad idea, and she raised them well. She divorced and remarried, ran a successful business, and traveled the world. She figured out how to work around her limitations, and family and friends came to understand that it was not okay to bring up the topic of polio around Joan.

Life was moving along according to plan when Joan started to show signs of weakness in her muscles and overwhelming fatigue. She became concerned. The doctors found that she was suffering from post-polio syndrome (PPS), which is a condition that can crop up in polio survivors anywhere from ten to forty years after recovery. PPS is characterized by a further weakening of the muscles that were previously affected by the polio infection.

Joan was shocked and in disbelief. After all those years of hiding her disabilities, now she would have to come face to face with all the emotions she had been so adept at burying. She knew she could not do this alone; she was going to need the help of her family, so she decided to call them all together and tell the story of what it had been like to contract polio all those years ago. She spoke with a counselor and steeled herself to tell her story at last. When the day came, she felt tremendously emotional. With tears streaming down her face, she recounted to her children and their spouses the story of the pain and weakness and fatigue she had experienced all those years ago. Joan wasn't sure what kind of response to expect, but it certainly wasn't the one she got!

What came pouring forth from her kids was not a lot of sympathy or relief but years of pent-up rage—all the hostility and anger they had had to keep bottled up because their mother refused to acknowledge her limitations. Joan felt totally overwhelmed by her family's response. Joan kept asking herself, What went wrong? Why was this happening?

As I sat and listened to Joan tell me her story my eyes filled with tears. I knew Joan's kids loved and admired her; that was obvious to all. Their mom had been such a go-getter all their lives. She was one of those women who could do everything and then some. Nothing could ever stop her. Joan's kids didn't know what to do with this new story about a life of pain and vulnerability. It was as if they didn't even want to believe her. As if all of those happy times had been some kind of charade.

It's tempting to wonder if things might have been different if Joan had told her story earlier, if her disabilities had been a more visible part of her everyday life. But the truth is, it doesn't really make any difference. Joan wasn't ready to tell the story until that moment, and everyone is simply going to have to figure out what to do with it. There are no mistakes. Joan will continue to tell the story of what is, and her children will come to understand that things change.

What Stops Us from Telling Our Stories?

There are all kinds of things that keep us from being able to see our own stories, let alone tell them. Sometimes it's fear of the unknown, fear that if we faced facts it might hurt too much, might be too terrible to bear. We don't want to burden other people with our pain, or we fear that our stories aren't *good enough* or *interesting enough*. Or we convince ourselves that everyone will laugh. We feel ashamed. The list of reasonable reasons goes on—and on and on. Trust me on this: No matter what has happened to you in life, no matter how painful or lucky or humiliating, you are not alone.

The Problem with Writing the Story Before Checking the Facts

I recently had a serious misunderstanding with my son. I knew I had been too brusque with him and had gone too far in telling him what I thought of his life, but now that it was out there, it was too late to take it back, and I was sure I had pushed him away for good. When I didn't hear from him in what I thought was a reasonable amount of time, I began to spin a dreadful fantasy of a permanent, unfixable rift.

I realize now that my fantasy was based on a childhood experience of what happens when family members fight: people go to their graves without reconciling. I had always thought of my son as a carbon copy of my brother Sam. Sam had left home as an adult over an argument with my mom and had never returned. My mom died without making contact with Sam, and I had seen how it had broken her heart. At some primal level, I was sure that was going to happen to me.

Because I didn't want to be the bossy interfering mother and I didn't want to make things worse or face rejection by reaching out to my son, I convinced myself that he would have to make the next move. As days passed, I grew sadder and sadder and the doomsday story grew larger and larger.

Thank the gods I had business to discuss with my daughter-in-law a few weeks after the rift began. When I reached her at work, the first thing she said was, "We were wondering when you were going to answer our e-mails!" I had been having trouble with my computer and hadn't been able to check e-mail for weeks, but in my anxious state it had never occurred to me that that's how they might have tried to reach me. Had I been willing to let our story unfold without fear, I can see now, I would have reached out weeks earlier and tried to mend the damage I'd done with my judgments and opinions. I also would have discovered that my son wasn't nearly as angry as I'd feared. Instead I caused myself needless suffering. It's amazing how making up stories in our head tends to separate us from each other. It could be about our son or our brother or who knows, but it's the making up of the stories without facts that gets us into trouble.

But some good came of this, too. Because I am learning that there are no mistakes and realized that I'd made up a story that had nothing to do with the real circumstances, I was able to share my fears with my son, and together we are writing a different story. I realized that I could drop the fear of being the bossy, interfering mother and just allow myself to be vulnerable. I'm sure I will always be just a little bit bossy and interfering—my kids wouldn't recognize me otherwise—but I think I learned from this that it's a good idea to remain open and curious about where a fear like that is coming from and to recognize it for what it is.

Of course I will continue to care, and sometimes that will get me into trouble and cause me pain. Especially for parents, there's often a very fine line between caring and controlling, but the best we can do is keep our eyes open.

Another, related, story has had an even fiercer grip on my life. It goes like this: I am a Wiley. I am strong. I am able to do it all; I will never show my vulnerability. It's too risky. My goodness, what an uncomfortable story to be part of! This is the story that supported my isolated drinking and loneliness. If I had still been rerunning this story in relation to my son, I would probably have been triggered to get out the bottle and drink myself to sleep to ease the pain. I am happy to say I am a grateful alcoholic and that did not happen.

Family Myths

One day I was telling a friend what had happened with my son. Somewhere around the part about my mother and Sam she just started to laugh and shake her head. "I guess all families are the same," she said, and then related a story about her brother and sister.

Each year her family would get together on Thanksgiving Day, and each year the tension between her brother and sister would begin to build the moment they'd both arrived. Their conversation was always superficial and guarded. During one of these get-togethers the subject of summer camp came up, and the root of the conflict between her brother and sister was finally exposed. Apparently when they were kids, her brother Joe had been sent off to a camp every summer. He hated it and was sure they sent him away because no one loved him and they just wanted to get rid of him. Her sister Jane, on the other hand, resented the hell out of Joe because he got to escape, whereas she had had to stay home and listen to her alcoholic mother rant and rave all summer long. For years no one ever talked about what it was like living with an alcoholic mother. Instead, Jane lived with her terrible jealousy of Joe, and Joe nursed feelings of being totally unloved. Each was hiding behind a wall of resentment. That is, until they stumbled on the subject of summer camp and realized how their misperceptions and misplaced anger had cost them years of closeness. Giving up resentment often allows us to hear our own story or that of another with an open heart.

Fear of Being a Burden

Sometimes we fear that telling our stories will burden other people or cause them discomfort. And sometimes they will, but we have to tell them anyway. A friend of mine had just lost her sister to cancer. She was sitting with some old friends one day when one shared a story of something wonderful her sister had done for her, and the others all chimed in, "Isn't it wonderful to have sisters? I can't imagine life without my sister," having apparently forgotten their friend's recent loss. My friend had the choice to sit there and endure it or say something. Saying something would likely make her friends uncomfortable, and maybe even a bit mad (for raining on their good time), but she decided that *not* saying anything would be worse. She spoke up and said she felt angry and invisible, and her friends did apologize for being insensitive. And they also seemed a bit annoyed at being called to task. However, we can't let the fear of being a burden stop us.

We All Have Valid Stories

My friend Andy had never been on vacation by himself, but he was at the end of his physical and emotional rope and needed a rest. Andy's younger brother was autistic and the family rarely talked about the toll this took on all of the family members. Andy felt terribly guilty as he boarded the plane to fly off into the sunshine. He wasn't sure he had the right to have fun while his family suffered.

During the five-hour plane trip, Andy got to talking to his seatmate. As luck would have it, she was a social worker on her way to a three-day seminar on family resources for families dealing with autism. Andy felt totally free to talk about how he was affected by his little brother's disability. He talked for a long time about the tremendous guilt he carried around because there wasn't anything he could do for his brother or his mother. The gift of this conversation with the social worker was learning that when one family member has a disability it affects the entire family. He realized that even though he didn't live in the same town as his mother and brother, he still absorbed a lot of the worry and was entitled to his own feelings and his own support.

As Andy learned that day on the plane, telling our stories has the potential to liberate us from the dreaded fear that we are all alone. Becoming comfortable with life as it is requires of us an acknowledgment of our need for support, of our fundamental interconnection. We may carry each other's burdens, but that means there will always be others to help us carry ours.

How Much Is Too Much?

Of course you don't want to become so enamored of your story that it's all you want to talk about. We all know people who bring every conversation back to them and don't seem to have attention for anything *but* their own stories. Or they have become so accustomed to embellishing their stories that they forget that the stories are not even true. It's very important to check in with yourself from time to time and make sure you haven't started telling tall tales. These can sneak up on you, too. You start embellishing, and pretty soon you are telling made-up stories because they get you a good response. From there it's a very slippery slope to forgetting who you are. It's important to remember that the purpose of telling your story is to sharpen your perception of yourself, to discover what's true, and to make connections with others who relate to your experience.

Owning Your Part

Most of us have the hardest time owning our own part in events where we felt the most wronged. We tend to hold on for dear life to our version of the story, the one where someone *did something* to us and we had no power to do anything at all. Go back and look again. Consider what that same experience might have looked like from the other person's perspective, or why they behaved the way they did. If you are willing to look at your own part, you may be surprised to see that you really did contribute to that outcome after all. Start with something simple, like the last time you went to work sick, pretending to everyone that you were just fine only to chop off the head of the first person to ask you for something you weren't prepared for. If that's not familiar, I'm sure you can think of a good example from your own life. It is always a good idea to ask yourself what part you might have played in the outcomes of difficult situations. Part of telling your story is the willingness to go back and amend a memory that no longer seems entirely whole and true.

Listening Is Part of It, Too

Of course there's more to sharing our stories than just telling. Part of the sharing is in listening to the stories other people have to tell.

Recently I had my patio redone. Every day Jose would show up with his truck full of tools and work at creating my beautiful new brick patio. I didn't know Jose before this; he was someone I hired to lay the bricks. One day, as he unloaded the bricks from his truck, I casually asked him how he was doing. With a big grin on his face he answered me with the most beautiful and enthusiastic, *"I am just fine!"* that I have heard in a long time. Then he told me the story of his liver transplant.

Six years earlier he had been diagnosed with liver disease, and he almost died. He was fortunate; a matching donor was found. He was weak and out of commission for months and months, but he made a full recovery. He still has to take medicine every day and will continue to for the rest of his life. But Jose learned in a very concrete way that each moment is all that we can be sure of and he truly appreciates each day. The fact that he can lift the bricks out of his truck, that he can sweat and labor to create my beautiful patio is something beautiful to him. His profound gratitude for life became part of my patio. Had Jose not told me his story, had I not taken the time to listen, I would have had a lovely but ordinary patio. Now I have a patio that stands as a constant reminder to me to be grateful, a patio that reminds me that each moment is all we have.

Every day we have the opportunity to share our stories and share the essence of who we are, how we live and learn. These stories can be guideposts that shine a light on the path we are walking.

Finding the Right Place for Sharing Your Pain

If you don't have people in your life with whom you can share your story, there are all sorts of groups out there, both online and live, that will support you. Whether a twelve-step group, a grief group, a group for people experiencing life transitions, a group that supports a particular aspect of who you are (Catholic, pagan, gay, a stay-at-home parent), there's a place for you and your story.

If you are in a very vulnerable emotional place, you might want to take a friend or family member along with you the first time you go to a group. And beware of any group or person who tells you they have *the* answer. When you tell your story and share the truth about your own pain, hurt, or vulnerability in a group setting, or wherever you tell it, you should not be made to feel wrong. Your experience is your experience. No right. No wrong. It just is.

When you first go to a group, you might want to start out by listening. Having the opportunity to listen to other people's stories often gives us the courage to hear—and tell—our own stories without guilt, shame, or fear. Listening with an open heart to the stories of others will often lead you to have compassion for your own true story when it is unearthed.

The Only Constant Is Change

Some years after my daughter Beth had died, another parent who had lost a child asked me how long it had taken me to get my smile back. I can still remember my answer: "I don't know; it just seems to happen in small bits and pieces." And that's how our stories change. There's really no such thing as the *whole* story, because the story is always changing, always evolving.

For several years after the death of my daughter I had a difficult time answering the question, "How many children do you have?" I didn't know whether I should say *three* or *two*. Saying, "I gave birth to three children but now I only have two," was certainly a conversation stopper, but not telling the truth seemed to dishonor both Beth and me. No matter what I said I felt that I was some how telling a lie. The silence that often followed the truth was unbearable. What I didn't realize early on was that I didn't have to tell the same story every time. Now I know that I can decide how to answer depending on how comfortable I feel. And I don't mind the silence so much any more. The only thing that's important is that I know and honor my own story.

Practice: Tell Your Story

1. Think of someone you trust and are comfortable with and to whom you'd be able to tell your story honestly, whatever part of it you feel like telling, be it something you've never shared before, or something that's been particularly troubling you. Just be sure it's something you feel ready to tell.

2. Decide on the parameters (and remember that you can change your mind): Do you want him or her just to listen and bear witness, or would it be okay if he asked questions or offered feedback? Will you need a promise of confidentiality, or would it be okay for that person to share your story with others? *Remember, you get to decide.*

3. Now, go ask that person if she or he would be willing to listen to your story.

4. If she or he says "Yes," go for it, and when you're done, think about how it felt: Was it as scary as you'd feared? Neutral? Exhilarating? Just sit with the feelings and reflect on what it feels like to open up and share.

5

Laugh at Yourself

As we navigate life, many of us have a tendency to take things all too seriously. We cling to what was and not let things unfold naturally. We think that if we just hang in there and remain on top of things, we'll be able to control what happens to us. One of the qualities I think I admire most about "comfortable" people is their ability to laugh at themselves—especially at the ways they try too hard to control outcomes.

Recently my friend Sandra's house burned down. That certainly was not funny, nothing to laugh at. Her community, including people she had known all of her life, some new acquaintances, and some total strangers who seemed to appear out of nowhere to help (or just to witness the amazing force of the fire) gathered around her in support. We all cried with her—some because they had played in the house as children, others because it was an historic house, others just at the sheer sadness of seeing someone's home go up in smoke—and then plunged right in to help her sort through the remains of the house.

And, unexpectedly, we found lots of things to laugh about. As we sorted through some old pictures, we laughed at the hair and clothes we'd thought were so glamorous back in the '50s. The laughter was a marvelous tonic.

I helped Sandra dig through the basement to find the treasures she had been keeping for her children and grandchildren. As we dug we came across a statue of Quan Yin, the Buddhist goddess of love and compassion. The statue's head was missing and she was covered with soot, but Sandra knew that Quan Yin was one of my favorite goddesses and asked if I would like to have her for my garden. I immediately said, "Yes, she will be my reminder of impermanence." I wrapped up the statue, took her home, and sprayed her with an acrylic spray. That's when I burst out laughing: Here I was attempting to preserve the look of impermanence! I was clinging to what is and not letting life unfold in a natural way.

One of the classic ways women express this refusal to allow things to be as they are happens around body image and size. And who can blame us? At every turn we are shown what we *should* look like. Of course, few of us fit the ideal and we know it. But we still try to fit into the mold. And sometimes we remember to laugh at ourselves for it.

I'm thinking of the time two of my friends were out shopping for new bras. Neither of them fit the Victoria's Secret image. One was a 38A and the other a 36DD. Ms. 38A was having a hard time finding something that fit, and as she left the fitting room to get another bra, Ms. 36DD called out to ask her to bring in a black bra like the white one she had been trying. As Ms. 38A was heading back toward the fitting room with both garments, a clerk came up to her and ever so discreetly said, "Do you know those bras are two different sizes?"

My friend looked up at her with a straight face and said, "I know." As she held up the 38A, she said, "This is what I always wear but I have always wanted to see what it felt like to wear one of these," and held up the 36DD. Everyone cracked up.

Years ago I went on a Buddhist retreat to learn about present moment practice. The teacher was about fifteen minutes late, and when she arrived she told the story of her delay. She had been rushing around trying to get ready, and her mind was already with the group. She headed out of the house, her arms full of things to bring to the retreat, and left without closing the front door. Fortunately she noticed the open door as soon as she put her armloads of stuff down on the back seat of her car, but as she tried to step away from the car she caught her long skirt in the door. And the car door automatically locked. So there she was. The keys were out of reach in the car, she was trapped, and it was getting later by the minute. Doing the only thing she could think of, she stepped out of her skirt and went back into the house in her underwear to get another set of keys. It all worked out just fine, but so much for present moment practice. Everyone burst out laughing.

Who couldn't relate to a story like that? How often do we find ourselves rushing around, with our minds in a thousand places, and forgetting the present? Even though this happened years ago, I remember the story as if it were yesterday. It's one of the stories I tell myself as a reminder to stay grounded, that laughter is a wonderful teacher, and that even our most revered guides do well to laugh at themselves sometimes.

Laughing on the Outside, Crying on the Inside

This is not to say that we should laugh off serious matters. Nothing is more disconcerting than laughter that covers up pain, laughter that is used to keep from acknowledging difficult feelings — the class clown who keeps everyone laughing to avoid being seen himself. Using laughter as a tool for comfort rather than a cover-up is what we're after here.

Further, the ability to laugh at ourselves allows us to see our ordinariness, our inability to control the world; it allows us to confront our misconceptions and own our foibles and mistakes without beating ourselves up for being imperfect.

Finding the humor in life is also a valuable skill when talking about things that are really grim. A touch of levity can make it possible for other people to hear about something painful, whereas hearing the unvarnished, grim truth might just be too much to bear. Again, the balance we want to achieve is to use the humor as a tool of comfort but not as a way to hide. You want it to act as a buoy or a tension diffuser. That ability to steer things out of the dark into a humorous direction is often a critical ingredient in success.

I want you to meet my friend Peter. He went to school with my kids, so that would make him about forty-four now. Peter was popular with all the girls, including my daughter, but he was also wild and crazy and a heavy drinker as a teenager. When he was twenty-one, he had a terrible auto accident that broke his neck and left him a quadriplegic. He was unable to do anything for himself and plunged into a deep depression—and stayed there for several years. Eventually, thanks to the right medication, a lot of therapy, family support, and an open heart, he not only came out of the depression but gained a zest for life he'd never had before. Nowadays, Peter no longer hangs around on street corners talking about how awful everything is (yes, he did do that for a while), but he doesn't keep it hidden either. When a conversation comes around to that time in his life, he is open and puts everyone at ease as he describes the botched suicide attempts he made. He reminds me of Inspector Clouseau, that wonderful Peter Sellers character in the *Pink Panther* movies, who is able to laugh at his own shortcomings without denying the seriousness of the situation.

As with everything else, with humor you have to use your judgment. It's just as important to know when not to joke as well. It's always best to reserve our humor for shining the light of truth on ourselves but not for brandishing a weapon against others. It's not pretty to make fun of others.

I Can Do Anything Better Than You Can

Back when I thought I could do everything, I offered to fold about 40,000 flyers for distribution during a political campaign. I said my son would help me. When the flyers were delivered, I panicked. There were a lot more boxes than I thought there would be! Stewart and I sat at the dining room table and got started. Thank God my husband came along. He took one look at the number of boxes and decided to do a time-and-motion study to see how long this job would really take. Turned out it would have taken the two of us eighteen days, working eight hours a day, to complete the job! The election would have been over before we had finished.

I was embarrassed, but I quickly called in the troops for help. The house was filled with volunteers the entire weekend, everyone folding away for democracy. I met some new friends that weekend, too—people who are still friends thirty-five years later. We laugh when we think about how and why we met.

That's the key. To be able to laugh at yourself. Just remember: There's a big difference between laughing with and laughing at. What might be funny to one person can be like a knife blade cutting the skin and drawing blood for another, so we have to be aware.

Start with yourself. See if, as you go through your day, you can find a few opportunities to let go of minor tensions or mishaps with a little laughter. Get in the habit of laughing at the little stuff and see if it doesn't help you let it go.

When you look into the mirror and notice that first chin hair, do you go crazy and start worrying about getting old, or do you laugh and start carrying a tweezers in your makeup case? When you notice that bald spot shining through at the top of your head, do you head straight for the hair transplant or let out a Friar Tuck chuckle, knowing that your costume will look more authentic next Halloween? Your decision.

It's easy to get swallowed up by little aggravations, but we owe it to ourselves to laugh at these minor woes when we can. I'll never forget teaching a beading class in the Balkans. A young woman named Maria was using tiny beads to make a choker necklace, and she was groaning and complaining about how difficult it was. I suggested she stop, but she said, "No, it's pretty!" When I then remarked that the beads didn't care if she was groaning and complaining but that she would probably remember the struggle every time she wore them, she cracked up. My guess is that instead of remembering the difficulty, she probably remembers the laughter whenever she puts on that necklace. I sure hope so.

Another wonderful example comes from one of my lip reading students. Lois came to my class because she was having problems with communication due to her hearing loss. She had gone to the doctor about some pain in her legs and swears she heard him tell her, "You are having spasms of the brain." Of course what he actually said was that she was having spasms of the vein, but she went home and reported to her daughter that she was having brain spasms. Her daughter panicked, wondering if her mother should continue driving. She called the doctor, and when she reported her mother's problem to the doctor, he laughed and of course set the record straight. When I asked her, "Well, weren't *you* worried when you thought it was your brain?" she laughed, shrugged her shoulders, and said, "I just figured at my age something had to start going wrong."

It's amazing how humor can make a difficult situation more bearable and allow us to avoid suffering. Traveling in other countries has given me an insight into what a difference a little laughter and a smile can do to defuse misunderstandings. I learned this the hard way.

Practice: Making Lemonade

Think about a troubling or difficult experience and see if you can find *something* in it to laugh about. Periodically reflect on difficult moments and try to find the humor in them. Believe me, there's no better balm for the soul.

When I was nineteen years old, I went to visit my sister and brother-in-law in Japan. This was before jets, and it took thirty-six hours to get there. Now remember, I was as naïve as they come. I had never traveled outside of New Jersey, except for one trip to Detroit with my mother, and here I was in a foreign land. We took a trip up to Mt. Fuji, where my sister had arranged a date for me. My date and I went for a swim in the rain, and when we returned to the hotel the maid indicated that I should follow her. She also brought along my date.

She took us to a room with a wonderful Japanese tub. And then she started to remove my bathing suit. I almost died. There was a man in the room with me, for God's sake! I tried explaining that he was *just* my date, but she spoke no English. I stood there clutching my bathing suit and trying to explain. Finally I just smiled, and with humor, led her to the door and shut it after her. No way was I going to get into this tub with no clothes on.

My date got a good laugh, too, and we ended up taking the bath together in our bathing suits, behind closed doors. When I returned home and told my mother what happened, she said, "Oh, Eleanor how could you!" as if I were going straight to hell. Even getting that close to removing my bathing suit was more than she could stand. I laughed as I assured her that nothing had happened, and I have laughed ever since every time I think of my shock and horror and how the only thing to do was laugh.

I am also reminded of the wedding that almost wasn't. A friend of mine, Michelle, was a war bride—as in World War II. She came to the United States to be married. During preparations for the wedding, Michelle's mother-in-law, Mimi, explained that she would have to have a blood test and that the doctor might have to give her a shot in the "fanny." Well, hearing that, my friend almost passed out. In Britain at the time, the word *fanny* was slang for a woman's private parts, and the misunderstanding almost ended the marriage before it started! Fortunately Mimi asked Michelle what was wrong. Michelle was so embarrassed she could hardly get the words out of her mouth. But when the two women realized what had happened, they both burst into laughter.

Laughter can heal many a misunderstanding. In fact, putting laughter into our lives can be one of the most healing things we do. My friend Sandra, the one you met earlier whose house burned down, and I were having a conversation one day about all the parking tickets we have gotten in our lives and how angry and upset we each used to get when we found one on our car. We were chuckling about how each ticket should be amortized over the number of times we have done the same thing without getting caught! The very next day she gave me a call and was laughing so hard I could barely understand her.

Sandra is the "Bargain Queen." She's always priding herself on all the money she saves. Still giggling, she told me about how, after we'd parted the day before, she had decided to make a quick stop at one of her favorite haunts, the Salvation Army. When Sandra pulled up in front there were no parking places, so she parked in a nearby driveway (it was already blocked and she had parked there a thousand times before). It turned out to be an excellent shopping day. Sandra found a brand new blouse and silk turtleneck and figured she'd saved about $60.

You've probably guessed what happened next. Yep, she came out of the store to find a $50 ticket in her windshield for parking in an illegal space.

In years gone by Sandra would have been furious, outraged, but now she just laughed, went home, and paid the ticket. So much for bargains.

Remembering to laugh, even in dark times, ensures that we not get too hooked on outcomes. There's an old song that goes something like this: "Let a smile be your umbrella on a very rainy day." It works on sunny days, too. It keeps you from squinting and distorting the picture. I invite you to give it a try.

6

Find Community

One of the most *un*comfortable experiences we can have in life is loneliness. Not aloneness, but loneliness, feeling disconnected from other people. In the first chapter we talked about honoring our roots and the communities we were born into, at least for what they gave us to work with! These communities—and there were often several: religious, social, work-related, school—helped form us, too. We may have loved or hated these ties, but they imprinted themselves, and depending on what our early experiences were like, some of us became natural joiners and some of us feel suffocated at the mere thought of joining anything. People who had wonderful early experiences of community often find becoming involved and a part of something as natural as breathing. But those of us who experienced community as stifling or rigid may attach a fierce value to *not* belonging. We may see community as clubbish or elitist. The trouble is, we are social animals, and part of our security and comfort in this world comes from belonging *somewhere*. We can't just stay unattached forever.

When you come right down to it, a community is nothing more than a group of people bonded by a common need, experience, attitude, or interest, and most of us move in and out of many communities as we go about our lives. Community can arise anywhere more than two people are gathered, whether at church or synagogue or mosque, at a grief or other support group, through your interest in photography, bicycling, books, bird watching, volunteering at a soup kitchen, whatever. Community is about people taking care of each other around shared interest. And what's so vital about communities is that they support the physical, emotional, *and* spiritual parts of us. Communities provide companionship, and that's a good enough reason to be a part of one, especially when you live far away from family or other ties. Communities are also places where skills and resources can be shared. When difficulties or problems arise and you belong to a given community, chances are there will be others around you to help share the burden.

Because of the class and culture I grew up in, I learned a set of social behaviors; I was taught to keep to myself about hurtful things, to keep my responses private. I never told my story or asked questions. But now that I live in a more socially progressive area. I have become part of a community that shares stories of both joy and sorrow without guilt. What a blessing. When I find myself falling back into my old ways of silence and isolation, I recognize that I can do something about it. I know that if I'm just willing to ask, someone will be there to walk beside me on my journey.

Where Do I Belong?

When we don't have community, we can feel isolated and lonely and get a skewed idea of the world. Back in the late 1960s my husband and I moved to England. I was like a fish out of water. I didn't know the slang or the customs. I would do the wrong thing in the marketplace, like taking my own apples off of the fruit stand. Invariably someone would scold me and I would feel humiliated.

Community can also act as protection from harm. Fortunately, it wasn't long before I was taken under the wing of a movement teacher at the school where I taught. She invited me into her community, and it was there that I learned the proper protocol for shopping in the market. Life became so much easier when I learned the rules. This was my first experience as a minority, and it was quite eye opening.

Sometimes circumstance brings us together in community (communities of parents of kids at the same school, breast cancer survivors, parents who've had a child die) and sometimes it is wholly by choice.

Some years ago I had the opportunity to join a community of people whose passports had been stolen. Needless to say this was again not a community I chose. At the consulate's office in Barcelona, Spain, a bunch of us milled around, sharing stories, asking each other where we were from. When it came my turn to pay for my passport, I handed over the credit card that had not been stolen, only to find that I had canceled the wrong card. There I was, with no money and no working credit card, when out of the crowd came a voice: "Don't worry. I will lend you 100 euros and you can send me a check when you get home." This community took care of me.

Practice: What Does Community Mean to You?

Whether we like it or not, we need each other. But some of us take to community more easily than others.

Take a few moments to think about what community is for you. Is it a feeling of connectedness? A group with whom to share your interests? Something that smothers you and robs you of your individuality? Have you had good experiences with community? Bad? What attracts you and what scares you?

Now, think of three ways you can nurture healthy community in your life. Commit to doing at least one of those things this week.

When Community Doesn't Work

We've all heard stories about seemingly benign communities that were actually cults or were overly restrictive of people's individual liberties. How can we be part of a community without becoming swallowed up by it? How do we retain our individuality? Our free will?

Many communities have lots of rules, and that doesn't work for everyone. For instance, I'm someone who will follow the rules if there are any. I can't *not* follow the rules. And if the rules of a given community don't work for me, I simply can't be a full part of that community. Other people have an easier time taking the good parts and saying "No" to the rest, but I just can't do that. If you are a rule follower, I suggest that you be careful about getting involved in a community that has a lot of rules. As much as we need to belong, we must also guard our free will fiercely.

By the same token, we must be willing to break ties with a community that is no longer serving us or has become too restrictive in the way it functions. Of course, we also have to guard against becoming dilettantes and flitting from one to another in search of some perfect reflection of who we are. But we have to respect our own values and our right not to live by rules that don't fit.

Finding the Right Nest

All that said, we must never give up on finding our place and seeking the connection of a community. Especially as we strive to become comfortable with life as it is, not as it *should* be, we need people in our lives whom we can trust to provide a safe place for us as we tell our stories, as we come to accept ourselves and work at surrendering to what is without giving up.

When I was in early recovery I went to AA meetings daily, sometimes twice a day. I did that for more than a year. Now I share my story of recovery each time I teach and am part of a spiritual community that supports my continued recovery. I know I can go back to AA any day I need to and I will be accepted with open arms. I always go to an early morning meeting on my AA birthday, for instance, and some of the same people that were there fifteen years ago are still there; that's what they need to do.

Some people feel that same embrace, that same acceptance when they go back to see family. I do not. It's all okay. In order to be comfortable, we each have to find the community we belong in, the one or ones that accept us as who we are. What I had to do was become comfortable with myself before I felt I really belonged anywhere. That was a hard one. It's easier to blame the communities than to own our own discomfort in our skin.

These days I also find myself more comfortable *not* belonging to some communities. It doesn't mean there's something wrong with me or with the community; we just don't fit.

Because I travel and teach I am invited into many communities, I am accepted as the teacher, I am trusted. This means I have the responsibility of being open and honest, of doing no harm. I take this very seriously. I respect and honor each community that has invited me in to teach. In return I always ask the people I work with to take in only what fits for them. They must be comfortable with what I have to say and never just swallow it hook, line, and sinker because I am the teacher.

Although I am honored to be invited into a variety of settings, I am always pleased to return to my home and the comfort and ease of being with my family and friends, the community I have built during the past forty years. Within my home community I know I can be whoever I am. I can share my fears and my dreams. I will be heard and supported.

It's the spontaneous gatherings that mean so much to me, especially the ones that happen when one of us is in need. Being able to accept each other's help and knowing that we don't have to pay it back and that we would (and do) all do this for each other. And that bond affects our kids, too. The ones who live out of town, for instance, know that if they want to plan a surprise party for Mom's sixty-fifth birthday, all they have to do is give one of the others of us a call and they'll get all the help they need.

In my community, we are all different, we have different interests and different needs, but we honor and respect those differences.

Kindred Spirits

Sustainable communities rarely just happen. You have to work at them. Each member contributes their own special something and there's always give and take involved.

Amazingly enough, my first experience of this kind of community started with vegetables. When our kids were small and we were busy figuring out how to feed the hoards, some of the women in our community came together to form a cooperative. We would go to the wholesale produce market and buy inexpensive, quality fruits and vegetables and distribute them among the group. We did this for years, meeting once a week. We rotated jobs and meeting locations, and pretty soon the talk that went on each week became just as important as the vegetables we bought.

By the time our kids were off to college and we no longer needed the veggie group, we had formed a very solid community, and I belonged. This community has helped me quit smoking and get sober. They have celebrated my kids' weddings and are there for me each time I return from a teaching trip. That is a glorious feeling. And I have been there to listen without judgment when a painful story needed to be told, or delivered chicken soup when someone was too sick to cook. We seem to have gotten in tune with each other's present moments, both in joy and sorrow. We have gotten over the need to pay each other back; each of us knows we will have our turn.

One of the group recently had abdominal surgery and could not walk as fast or as far as the group, but she still shows up for our walks and we all slow down for her, take her around the block, and send her on her way to rest. She commented, "It is difficult for me to slow down and just do things as I can." Thank God for her community. They don't make it any easier to accept limitations; they allow her to recognize her own limitations and figure out how to take care of herself.

No one tries to be the fixer. We care for each other when the need arises and celebrate joyous occasions, but we are also there to be present with pain.

May we all find communities that nourish us so well.

7

Take Care of Yourself

We live in a society that prides itself on multitasking, on doing as many things at once as we possibly can. We tend to think we don't have time for anything else. But it's a choice we make. How can we notice ourselves or take our needs seriously when we don't make the time to notice what we're really doing? How many of us drag ourselves to work when we have a bad cold, only to pass the cold to our officemates? Who are we serving? No one.

When you think about putting yourself first, do you automatically think, "That would be selfish"? Do you turn yourself inside out to put other people first? Or are you able to recognize that the word *No* is a complete sentence and not take on too many activities?

When I meet people who are comfortable with life as it is, one of the things I notice is that they take good care of themselves. Not just eating right or working out, but putting their own needs up front and making sure they are okay before trying to take care of anyone or anything else.

Think about how often you hear the word *stress* these days, and almost always in a negative context. "This is so stressful," "that's so stressful." If we continually reinforce the negative aspects of stress, of course it makes an impact. But stress has other aspects as well. A friend from India appears to be comfortable with life in the midst of an amazingly busy schedule. I might call it stressful, but he seems to float right through it unruffled. When I asked him how on earth he does it, he said, "This is the time in my life when I am supposed to be busy and making a living for my family." Stress is not a word in his regular vocabulary. He does not get stressed; he is just busy. This is a philosophy he was brought up with; he does not have an expectation of things being any other way. When I enter his house, he treats me as the most important person in the world. A sense of calm and well-being always prevails.

It is up to us how we relate to our busy-ness. We can create stress in our minds, which then moves into our bodies, or we can decide we are simply busy (or we can get less busy!).

Years and years ago I wrote a paper on stress. What stayed with me from my research is the fact that there are both good and bad stressors. If we pile up too many stressors, positive or negative, we set ourselves up to become sick. We all have limits, and if we don't recognize them, we are headed for trouble. Even if things are great in your life, you still have limits. Unfortunately, trouble often doesn't rear its head until the damage is permanent. But if we pay attention we can reverse the damage. It's all up to us.

Drinking, smoking, overeating, not sleeping—you name it. We each have our own weak spot that we tend to ignore. I used to be a smoker, and I know that if I picked up a cigarette today I would be a smoker again. I tried to quit three times before it stuck. I always found excuses to start up again. That's because I was always quitting for someone else. When I finally decided to stop smoking as a fiftieth birthday present *to myself,* it worked. During the interview for the stop smoking program I chose I was asked the question, "Are you under any stress at the moment?" My answer was "Yes"—a young friend was dying. The interviewer suggested that I not begin the program until things were smoother, but I decided to go ahead. I knew that if I waited until there was no stress in my life I might never quit, and Kurt, my sick young friend, who was undergoing a bone marrow transplant, was cheering me on all the while.

I gave myself the gift of no smoking, and I also gave it to Kurt. I let my friends and the staff at the program take care of me. I couldn't have done it without help, and it was a big favor to ask. I quit smoking on March 17, 1987, and Kurt died May 7 of that same year.

I'm talking about taking the time to notice what you need and then making it a priority.

The Effects of Our Starter Kits

How we are brought up is a big influence on how we view taking care of ourselves as we walk through life. I was very fortunate to have a mom who took a nap every day after lunch. The house practically had to be burning down before anyone would think of going into her room between one and two o'clock. That was her rest time. She also had a group of lady friends who had great fun together but also supported each other in times of need. Mom traveled every other year with a friend and visited each of her children once a year. She visited her doctor regularly and was faithful with her diet and medications for her high blood pressure.

Life was not always easy for my mom. My father lived with another woman while still married to my mom (that story merits a whole book of its own), but she raised nine kids (some not so easy) and somehow managed to keep some balance in her life. She was a wonderful role model for me. I learned how to manage, and I also learned what I didn't want to do with my life. I wasn't going to have a husband who fooled around on me.

As an adult, I longed to be as comfortable with life as my mom seemed to be with hers. It has taken me years of floundering and hard work, but I think I have come to that place of being comfortable with my life as it is. Sometimes I lose that sense of comfort for a time, but I know what I need to do to take care of myself and stay balanced. Most of us were not raised to take care of ourselves, and many people, especially women, even find it difficult to *think* about such a thing. It seems so selfish and irresponsible and goes against all our conditioning. Now don't get me wrong. I'm not suggesting becoming a complete narcissist or egomaniac or setting yourself above everyone else, I just mean recognizing your needs and taking care of them-like my mom did with her naptime—so that you have a self to give. Just like when you fly you're always told to put on your own oxygen mask first before helping anyone else, it's about being practical and safe.

Practice: A Half-Hour Just for You

Take a half-hour to be alone and unplug. Turn off the ringer on the telephone; shut down the computer, TV, and radio; and do one of the following:

- Nap
- Read a book
- Eat some ice cream
- Sit in a garden
- Take a bath
- [Fill in the blank!]

Now try giving yourself a half-hour *every day* to take care of yourself. No matter how out of control your life may seem, you *do* have the time. Find it, and give it to yourself. You deserve it.

Most of us are out of practice at taking the time to notice what we are feeling and what we need, and it *is* at the core of becoming comfortable with life as it is. You have to befriend your inner guide and trust your gut feelings.

I once talked with a young woman who had a brace on her leg about this whole business of gut intuition and taking care of ourselves. I hadn't met her before; we were on a hiking trail together and I couldn't help but notice her brace—it was hot out and we were wearing shorts. Because I am nosy I asked if she had a drop foot and what had caused it. She very easily told me the story of the brain surgery she had undergone and the disabilities she was left with. She had worked in the health care field so she was aware of neurological symptoms. Blurred vision and tingling in her arm sent her off to the doctors, but by the time she got her appointment the symptoms had subsided and the doctor gave her a clean bill of health. Something in her gut told her this wasn't right but she didn't question it outright. A few months later the symptoms reappeared and she insisted on an MRI, which showed that she had a bleeding aneurysm. She was immediately sent to the operating room for surgery, where the bleeding was stopped, but she was left with paralysis and memory loss.

While in rehab, she told me, she was taken care of by some former students. She said she found that she actually liked being a patient and discovering what it was like "on the other side" of the therapist-patient team. It gave her a whole new understanding of suffering, of the courage and work that is needed on the road to recovery.

One of the things she mentioned, too, was that she doesn't remember how hard she struggled in the early days of her recovery. She has had a kind of blackout of that whole experience and relies on the stories told by her family and caregivers, who talk about the incredible courage and fortitude she displayed during those early days. I told her about my own recovery from alcoholism and how it was having blackouts and not knowing what I had done while I was unconscious that jolted me into the knowledge that I needed to get sober and take better care of myself. We remarked on how our very different paths had both brought us to some of the same realizations: that it was okay to ask for help and necessary to take good care of ourselves to prevent a recurrence or relapse. We were able to laugh together about the frustrations of not knowing what we had done in the past and how sometimes you have to trust both yourself and others and just surrender to what is.

Recently the doctor asked this woman to keep track of any weakness she experienced during a two-week period. It drove her crazy. She hated having to dwell on what was wrong rather than what was right with her life. But she also understood how important it was to acknowledge symptoms of decline and what they might mean. She works daily to create a balance between paying attention to and ignoring changes that occur in her physical abilities.

Getting Help When You Need It

One of the ways my new friend celebrated her steps toward recovery was by putting away her brace. But now she also accepts that she needs it on certain days, like the day we met on our hike on uneven terrain. It's a matter of safety. If she didn't wear the brace, she wouldn't be able to hike, and that's not a choice she wants to make. Because she has learned how to take care of herself, it's okay to put the brace back on and not see it as a setback.

I think about my own experiences with asking for help not as a sign of weakness but as a way of taking care of myself. About ten years ago, when I started doing a lot of traveling for my prayer bead work, I could easily get my own heavy bags on and off the carousel. Now I spend the money and have a Skycap do it for me. And, as I mentioned earlier, these days it's also easier to honor my need for solitude following a workshop. I don't feel guilty turning down invitations anymore. No matter how well meaning other people may be, we need to be clear with them about what we need to properly care for ourselves. If we don't tell people what we need, they will give us what they think we need, and often there isn't a match. When this happens we just have to be willing to talk honestly and work it through.

Surrendering to Our Need for Help

Surrendering to the fact that we can't do it all or carry it all and accepting help is often the best way to take care of ourselves.

I have a young friend who is bipolar. She sees a therapist twice a month. She told me she will probably have to do this for the rest of her life. This young woman is very fortunate and has great courage. She has embraced her mental illness and has learned at a young age how to care for herself. She knows how awful it feels to have a bipolar episode and she never wants to have another one. She takes care of herself, takes her medication, makes sure she gets proper rest. She now holds down a challenging job and has a wonderful family life.

Learning that we are responsible for taking care of ourselves can be a very tough lesson. I don't mean that others don't help us—of course they do—but the willingness to let ourselves be cared for and to ask for help has to come from us. As a parent, for example, I can't stand seeing my children suffer. If something's going wrong, I want to fix it for them. It's so hard to sit with them when they are in pain and not take charge. But I know all too well that I wouldn't be doing them any favors to rescue them from their problems. They need to find their own way through struggle. What I can do is be present for them and offer help when it's asked for.

Being Present for Others

It may seem ironic that the most comfortable people I have met are the ones who know they can't fix the world. They can only fix themselves, and they are able to be present with someone else's pain without necessarily *doing* anything. In some circles chronic fixers are called "codependent." Oh, it's such a delicate balance, being open and willing to care for each other without becoming codependent, taking care of ourselves when we can, taking responsibility for our own health and not expecting a pill, a doctor, or a magic charm to fix us. You know that old saying about burning the candle at both ends? We have to make peace with the fact that if we eat 6,000 calories a day we will gain weight, that if we only get four hours of sleep a night we will be tired and may jeopardize our health. It is up to us to make the choices that support our health.

It's all about taking a look, a clear look, at how we live our lives, and coming to a sense of peace about who we are. Are you an introvert or an extrovert? Do you require a little sleep or a lot? What kind of exercise works for you? Is there a medication that will ease your pain? This is not a one-size-fits-all world. Each of us has to figure out what works for us. If you are fortunate, there may be many people who can help, but ultimately you are the only one who knows what works for you. And then it's up to you to speak up or make the choices that put you first.

8

Know How to Put Yourself Together Again After Things Fall Apart

Like so many people I know, I was programmed to hold it together no matter what the cost, to put on a good face and look like I could handle anything, even if I was dying inside. For years it was drilled into me that looking good to the world was the most wonderful trait anyone could possess. And I spent a lot of years putting every ounce of energy into keeping it all together. Looking competent and capable. What was the alternative? Falling apart sometimes. I guess a lot of us think the world will stop turning if we aren't there to see that it continues spinning on its axis. There's that old illusion of control again.

Some of us can't even allow ourselves to stay home in bed when we have a cold. And sometimes our determination to keep it together is so fierce that it even withstands life's earthquakes. My daughter Beth's death, at the age of three, was one of those earthquakes if there ever was one. But it took me years to admit that her death unraveled me. To any and all who asked, I would insist, firmly, that I was okay.

My husband, my kids, and I were crumbling inside, but we had so much to do. Frankly, I wouldn't have even known *how* to fall apart. Back then, there were no support groups or books for parents whose children had died. Everyone just suggested that I get back to normal as quickly as possible. But there was no normal for me. People avoided us; no one talked about our beautiful little girl. The funeral director even had the temerity to comment, "You will have to look at the large caskets and then we'll order a small one, *because children don't die.*" I didn't scream, I didn't hit him. In fact I think I just carried on as if it didn't bother me, but I know that I was crumbling inside.

I took down all of Beth's pictures. I "got on with things." I walked around in a stupor for along time. This was nothing I had ever dreamed would happen to me.

Nothing gave me solace. I tried talking to my priest, and his advice was to have another baby. I wanted to scream, but did I? Of course not. I kept it together because it was inconceivable to fall apart. I continued to go to church because that was what I was supposed to do, but now it was empty for me. I couldn't talk to anyone there. I couldn't really talk to anyone. My husband and I were just going through the motions. He was devastated. Beth was his special girl; she had been born on his birthday. We each had our private sorrow that we were unable to share. We were falling apart but made believe that we were getting back to "normal."

When the housing protests over race discrimination began during that summer in my hometown of Alameda, I jumped at the chance to participate. I thought things would get back to normal if I could work toward solving the problems of others. And in a funny way I was right. Without realizing it, I had taken the first step toward healing. I was at least looking at pain, even if it wasn't my own. It would take years before I could look inside and be present with my own pain and loss, but this was the first step.

Several years later, when I participated in one of Elizabeth Kübler-Ross's seminars on death, I had to take a look at the old wounds, the ones I had covered over in order to carry on. I realized that grieving a daughter's death *was normal*—and a very slow process. It's a life-long process.

I am no longer in a state of constant grief about my daughter, but the pain of her death is never very far away. It can be triggered easily by someone I meet or something I see on television. But now I can also share the gifts her death gave me. Yes, there were gifts. I came to know, in a very concrete way, that all we have is this moment. There are no guarantees beyond this, and that is not a bad thing. In fact, it is very freeing. It makes life vibrant.

I also came to accept that none of us gets out of life without dying, and now I can freely speak about it and no longer dread talking about Beth's death. And I came to appreciate my other children in a very special way. I no longer take *them* for granted—ever.

We all fall back into self-doubt and inner turmoil from time to time. But people who have become comfortable with life as it is have some tools for digging themselves out of the pit. They may fall down, but they know how to get up. They may have pain or worry or problems, but they know how to pull out of their distress, and they have the capacity to *choose* not to suffer.

My road to becoming comfortable with life as it is has had many twists and turns, and there have been a few more earthquakes, though thankfully none of the same magnitude as the first. But part of it involved the profound learning that it's okay to fall apart. . . . And I *will* get back up again.

My drinking was another kind of falling apart, but it came upon me slowly and pretty much in secret. The few times I showed public drunkenness, like the time I drove my car into a bus stop while in a blackout, people made excuses for me. *She's just tired. She must have gotten drowsy in that hot tub.* I stumbled along for several years keeping my drinking a secret, putting on a good face for the community. Then I decided to go to graduate school to become a hospital administrator and soon discovered that I couldn't drink and study at the same time. So I stopped drinking, except on Sunday. I didn't stop because I thought I was an alcoholic, I stopped because I couldn't concentrate on my schoolwork.

Eighteen months later, I completed my MS in hospital adminis-tration—and started drinking again. I still hadn't come to the under-standing that I was an alcoholic. Fortunately, a friend from school had introduced me to meditation, and the practice would eventually help me see myself more clearly. Alcoholism is a disease that contin-ues to progress even if you stop drinking for a while, and progress it did. Seven months after getting my degree, I finally admitted I was a drunk. Oh, how people hated to hear me say that about myself! Some of them still do, sixteen years later. The point is, I could not begin the long process of getting back up until I was willing to fall apart and admit that I was an alcoholic.

I have been sober for sixteen years, but I still have to be very care-ful about my addictive personality. I have to watch myself carefully because I can get addicted to pretty much anything—having toast for breakfast each morning, saying prayers, walking five miles a day, drinking coffee. Actually, I drink everything like there is no tomor-row—water, hot coffee, soda, you put it in front of me and it's gone. The one that gets me into trouble is the coffee. I have burned the roof of my mouth more times than I can count. Now you would think that would teach me. I *am* slightly better, mind you, when I remem-ber to pay attention to what I'm doing. That is the trick: noticing what we do.

Falling down and getting up again is one of those things that hap-pens throughout life. If we notice, if we pay attention, we can sit down and rest, regain our energy, and then get up again. If we just blunder on, we might find ourselves on the ground and not remem-ber how we got there.

When you stumble and fall, do you notice what happened and stop to rest, or do you just get up and walk and ignore the pain?

Practice: Finding Your Anchor

No matter where you are emotionally right now, think about what anchors you when things are falling apart. What helps you regain stable ground? Certain people? Certain places or rituals? Breathing? Meditation? A walk? Write them down and keep the piece of paper handy. Now, commit to practicing these when things are good, so you'll be equipped next time things fall apart—and they will.

Azim: The Road to Forgiveness

We are remarkable creatures in that we can suffer enormously and still get up again. Several years ago I had the opportunity to hear a man named Azim Khamisa speak about forgiveness at a conference on attitudinal healing. Back in 1995, Azim's son Tariq was murdered by a fifteen-year-old boy over a pizza. I had a hard time believing him when he said he had forgiven Tony, the boy who murdered his son. That just seemed over the top to me. I know the pain of a child's death and the painful journey to wholeness. How could he forgive? I needed to know more.

So I purchased his book, *Azim's Bardo: From Murder to Forgiveness*. I wanted to understand; I wanted to know about the tools he used to get back up after this terrible fall. I was astonished. As Azim saw it, there were victims at both ends of the gun used that night; two boys were lost. He described how he came together with the murderer's grandfather to grieve and to work together to stop violence in our schools.

Over the years, I've thought a lot about Azim, Tony's grandfather Ples, and Tony. I often tell their story when I teach. I've been curious where the path of forgiveness has taken Azim over the years. I wanted to know what effect telling his story over and over had on him. And so, recently, I contacted the foundation that had sponsored the conference to see how I might get in touch with him.

As it turned out, Azim was scheduled to be in the Bay Area for another conference soon after my call, and he needed a ride from the airport to his hotel. I offered to pick him up. It was a beautiful sunny morning as we drove past San Quentin, the federal prison that sits just outside San Francisco and a huge symbol of what we do with violent men. *This,* I thought as we drove past, *is where our children will end up if we cannot stem the violence when they are young.*

Our conversation was easy. Azim told me that the next day would be the tenth anniversary of Tariq's death. "When Tariq was murdered," he continued, "a huge painful wound was opened in my heart. He was my only son. I thought it would never heal. Each time I tell my story it is like I remove the scab. It is painful and it bleeds. But when it heals over the scar is a bit smaller. My heart was about the size of a pea in those early days, the pain overwhelming. But each time I tell my story my heart grows a bit larger; perhaps one day my heart will be bigger than the scar."

I knew as he spoke that he truly understands that all we have is each moment. Although we can never bring back his son, we can work against youth violence. Azim allowed himself to fall apart, to grieve, but then decided to channel some of his grief into action. His hope is that by speaking out, he is making a difference. What matters is not vengeance but that his son's death *mean* something to others.

We talked about many things that morning, including how people who do *not* get knocked down are able to grow. Having been to hell and back, we both expressed our gratitude at having been given the grace to see life differently. But we wondered if we would have woken up to life without the experience of falling down.

As I have gained the courage to talk about Beth's death, as I have gotten comfortable with the idea that any one of us can be gone in an instant, death no longer depresses me. Falling and getting back up has given me great courage—to tell my story, to teach people about peace and diversity, to be present with other people's pain, just to be present with what is. I know I will be okay, no matter what happens.

Of course, it isn't necessary to be knocked down by death to wake up to the world. Any number of experiences can be a wake up. I recently visited my daughter's old friend Peter, the man who had bounced back from the terrible depression he'd suffered after his auto accident. I had arranged to see him when I discovered that he lived in a college town I would be visiting for a workshop. Until that morning, I had never thought I would hear from a paraplegic that his accident, "was the best thing that could have happened to me." But Peter was awakened to life and to his own gifts by his accident, and he means it when he says it saved his life.

I asked him what turned things around, and he told me that it was only when an old girlfriend finally got him to Easter Seals and some rehab that he started down the road to recovery. In the rehab setting, people no longer bombarded him with reminders of what he had lost in the accident but instead honored each advance he made. They appreciated his wit and his sense of humor. They saw him as a capable young man who happened to need an electric wheelchair to get around. Through rehab and a lot of hard work he regained minimal use of his arms, but he was not able to regain use of his legs and was confined to a wheelchair. But with the bolstering he got from that experience, he enrolled in college and started using his brain instead of his brawn.

As he made gains he realized that he really needed to get away from his old crowd, who were going nowhere. He had a sister in the Southwest and the college near her had an accessible program for people with special needs, so off he went, never looking back.

Peter has since had many adventures, even sky diving. Paying attention to detail, being in the present moment, doing one thing at a time have become a way of life for this man. It's the only way to go when you are a paraplegic. Being in his presence, even for just a few hours, I was struck by the sense that I could learn a lot about life from him.

Sure, there are things he longs for—a wife and family, for starters. He feels too unsure to pursue a romance; he worries about rejection and spoke of this with sadness. He wishes his dad could have lived long enough to see his graduation from college and knows how proud he would have been. And he gets tired of paying attention, but, as he says, that's just life.

He also has his setbacks. The helper dog that gave him so much assistance died several months ago and threw him into a slump, during which time he didn't pay attention to his body, and he got a bad pressure sore. But he used the time in recovery to assess what *is* in his life. Instead of staying in a blue funk, he looked at what he needs to do to stay as independent as possible and comfortable with his life, a life he has come to dearly love and appreciate. He will be getting a new dog soon; he will enter graduate school in the fall; he will continue seeking new adventures.

When the accident happened, many of us thought it might be kinder if his parents and the doctors just let him go, but Peter's mom fought for his life tooth and nail. Too bad she isn't here to see what a wonderful man her son has become. He hasn't entirely lost his bravado, but it's been tempered by a healthy dose of humility and courage. And that's a great combination.

The fact is, in life, stuff happens. Things fall apart sometimes. We all know that. But when the life you know disintegrates under your feet, how do you find stable ground? When life whacks you in the head, can you make the necessary repairs?

We can't always foresee the crises that will befall us, we can't always anticipate. And that's probably a very good thing, or we'd all be walking around waiting for the sky to fall. But we *are* responsible for how we respond when life gives us a whack. We may not be able to control our fate, but we are in charge of our reactions.

We may need time to regroup before we can even start on the road to recovery. We may have to sit for a long time with the changes and come to a place of acceptance. But then it's up to us to choose. Even in the most difficult situations, we can choose not to get bogged down. And sometimes the best thing we can do is sit still and mark time until we have the strength to move forward. The point is, moments of joy can always been found when we accept what is.

9

Be WIlling to Change Your Mind

Our starter kits always play a big role in whether we feel comfortable changing our minds. Many of us learned that changing your mind was a cardinal sin.

It has been a long, hard struggle for me to learn that it is alright to change my mind. I have always been prone to making snap decisions, which, once made, I thought I had to stick with to the death. In my family the rule was, once you said "Yes" to something or took a stand, you didn't change your mind unless it was literally going to kill you.

I can't tell you how many parties and movies I've gone to or committees I've joined because I initially said "Yes" and then didn't know how to change my mind. I would have all these resentments about the time I was wasting but then not be able to say I had made a mistake or changed my mind. I lived that pattern for a good number of years.

I envied people who could change their minds or were able to say "No" easily. I always felt the need to explain why I could not do something. When it was absolutely necessary to change my mind, I would apologize all over the place. Get the picture? It was a struggle. But one of the things I've noticed again and again about people who are comfortable with life as is it is that they give themselves permission to change their minds. It may not always be easy for them, but they do it. They do not stay in the same job, marriage, or religion if the cost-physical, mental, spiritual—is too great.

Giving oneself permission to change jobs, leave a bad marriage, or follow a different practice or spiritual path can open doors we never dreamed of. Take writing this book, for example. Had I not been willing to change where and how I worked, I would still be at the hospital treating patients. I would not have traveled around the world with my prayer wheel, hearing and telling stories, and I would not have had the experiences that I write about in this book. Was it easy giving up a steady job with a regular income? Of course not. Was I scared? You bet. I still get scared from time to time, but learning to stay open and flexible, and not to have rigid expectations, has opened a wide, wide world to me. The way I live now is not as I had pictured it years ago. And I love it. Give flexibility a try; you might like it, too.

My friend Agnes and her husband provide another perfect example. I have watched more than once as they have had to change their minds on major decisions. They seem to do it with such ease. Early in their marriage they surrendered to the fact that life is not what they thought it would be. When I first met them, Agnes was working as a hospital technician and, in addition to their own girls, they had several foster children. They provided emergency shelter, so you never knew how many children you would find in their house on any given day.

They felt it was their mission in life to care for children in need, but their house wasn't big enough for too many kids, so they decided to buy a larger house. Their dream was to open a group home for foster children. Just around that time, a twenty-six-room boarding house came on the market. They thought it would be perfect. It was a real stretch financially. They scraped together every penny they had, and they got the house. There were some boarders already there, and the income from the boarders helped Agnes and Philip make their mortgage each month.

In order to open a group home, they had to apply for a child care license, and every person living in the household would need an FBI clearance. Agnes knew that if she applied for the FBI clearance, several of her boarders (who had been politically active or wouldn't pass clearance for other reasons) would move out, and she and her husband couldn't afford that loss of income. So here they were with a twenty-six-room house and no way to do what they had planned. Now what? Their only choice was to make more money, and that meant giving themselves permission to change their minds. And change their minds they did.

Room by room they fixed up the house and turned it into a bed and breakfast. For about ten years, Agnes kept her day job, getting up every morning, fixing breakfast for her guests, going to work for the evening shift, keeping everything moving. Her health was suffering; she could no longer work two jobs. So again she had to give herself permission to change her mind.

This time she gave herself permission to become a full-time innkeeper. That took a great leap of faith. Twenty-five years later, she and her husband realize that running a B&B is just another way of serving people in need. Retirement is now on the horizon, and the B&B is for sale. Although Agnes and Philip plan for the future, they both know that they can change their minds and direction at any time. It makes for great adventure and surprise. Who knows what doors will open down the line?

Start with the small stuff. That way you'll get a chance to develop the tools to deal with the big stuff when it comes along. And it will. That's one of those certainties of life, and giving yourself permission to change will help you through.

The next time you come home from the store with something you don't really like, return it. Sure, it means another trip to the store and that takes time, but give yourself that time. It feels good. The next time you've got plans for the evening but get home too tired, call your friends and bow out gracefully. You don't want to become a chronic canceller, but there's nothing wrong with once in a while telling your friends you can't make it. You don't even have to give excuses. Just give *yourself* the option of changing your mind. The world won't come to an end.

The Price of Stubbornness

Sometimes our stubbornness and inflexibility can cause us great pain and suffering. I practically had to get banged over the head with a brick to see the error of my ways. When I was in my early fifties I decided I needed a job that paid retirement benefits. I had been in private practice for most of my adult life as a speech pathologist, and that did not give me a consistent income. I gave myself permission to go to graduate school to get my master's degree in hospital administration. I was scared stiff. I had tried this twice before and never completed the work.

I chose a program that did not require a Graduate Record Exam because I was sure I would not pass it. It had been years since I'd been in school, and I didn't know anything about computers; I also had to learn how to use the library all over again. But I gave myself permission anyway. While I was in school, I gave myself permission to change my job, becoming an assistant hospital administrator. Giving up my practice as a speech therapist took a great deal of thought. I would no longer be able to work with people on a one-on-one basis, which I loved, but I rationalized that with hospital administration I would still be in long-term care; it would not be so different. Little did I know.

With great discipline and anguish, I finished the program. I was so proud of myself. I now had MS after my name. That was a good decision. It was good that I stuck with the suffering and pain of it and worked through to completion. But very quickly I discovered that I hated being a hospital administrator. I didn't get to spend enough time with the old people. I had to hire and fire staff. But I kept doing the job because that was the decision I had made, and the retirement benefits would take care of me in my old age.

After two years on the job, I developed a pain down my back and around my waist. I ignored it until I couldn't stand it anymore. I asked the head nurse to look at it, and she said she thought I had shingles. Shingles is a painful disease, and it was very hard on my emotions. The doctor (yes, I finally went) explained that shingles can be treated if caught early enough, but I had ignored it for too long. I just had to wait it out.

I spent the next several weeks lying on the floor, compresses on my back to ease the pain, in tears, thinking, *How do I get out of this mess?* And then I decided to quit my job.

Sometimes I wonder what would have happened if I had not gotten shingles. I might still be a miserable hospital administrator, sticking by my decision to have a regular retirement income.

I Can See Clearly Now

For me, it was getting sober that allowed me to become more comfortable with the idea of changing my mind. I pay much more attention to the journey than to what might happen in the distant future. I do plan, but I am willing to change direction when needed. I still fall into a panic about money and old age from time to time, but now I'm able to look at the decisions I make in a new light, the light of today and *what is*. I don't always have to fill my head with the stories about *what if*.

Little did my friend Peggy know, when she was plowing through her engineering books in college, where she would end up. In school, she was sure she would be creating amazing highways. Her creations are amazing, but highways they are not. Although her degree is in highway engineering, Peggy creates beautiful flower arrangements for conferences and trade shows. To put herself through college, she took a job with a florist and fell in love with the art. Just out of college, she took a job as an engineer. Her husband hated the long hours and the fact that she was always busy working during holidays and celebrations. But Peggy felt that she had earned this degree and was supposed to do something with it. Could she really give herself permission to take the road paved with beautiful flowers instead?

When the opportunity came along to decorate a trade show, she leaped at it. And things just flowed from there. She gave herself permission to follow her heart, and each time I see her work it brings a smile to my face. She gave herself permission, and look where it has taken her.

I recently traveled to Spain both for work and pleasure. As the work portion of the trip was ending, I was mugged, and my wallet and passport were stolen. I was really shaken by the mugging, but at first didn't want to admit it. I tried to stay on in Spain, but I could not get comfortable. I felt vulnerable and scared all the time. I had wanted this trip for a long time and my stubborn desire to see it through almost got the better of me. But, even though I had planned to vacation there for three *weeks*, I decided to go home, where I would feel more safe and supported, and take care of myself. I was willing to change my mind, and I'm very grateful that I was.

Sometimes people worry that changing their minds means their first decision was no good. They are afraid of leaving their safety zones. Some people make decisions easily and then feel stuck with them; some people take their time making decisions and feel stuck with them; oftentimes it's our fear of making a mistake, or of being seen as having made a mistake, that makes us unable to admit that we'd like to change our minds.

We worry, *If I change my mind will people stop taking me seriously? If I change my mind will I have to go back and start over? If I change my mind, will I look silly?*

It Takes Courage to Change Your Mind

Mary, the older of two children, grew up in a small valley town. Her parents were social workers involved in their church and community. She learned about social justice at home, led an active social life in her church youth group, and was the apple of her parents' eyes. She went off to school in Berkeley, a straight A student.

Being in Berkeley was a profound wake-up. She started to learn about the world and was continually meeting different kinds of people—rich, poor, black, white, gay, straight. Mary stayed well within her comfort zone and became very active in the Methodist church group on campus, which was mostly white and straight. Most of her social life revolved around this group.

By the time graduation rolled around, she was in a committed relationship with a young man, and they went off to New York City together to teach in an urban school. As much as Mary had been exposed to different cultures and lifestyles in Berkeley, New York still blew her mind. Once again she joined a church and became part of the community, but this church was a true urban church and welcomed everyone. All those "different" people she had met in Berkeley were an integral part of her church community here. Something started to shift inside her, but she didn't really understand what was going on.

Then, for spring break, she and another female teacher took a vacation to an island in the Caribbean. Much to her surprise, Mary fell in love with the other teacher. This was not part of her plan. She knew the word *lesbian,* but that was about all. It was certainly not something she ever thought about growing up. She had always dated men and been sure she would get married and raise a family one day. Needless to say, she was confused.

She was also afraid. Changing her mind about her sexuality and being in love with a woman was okay in New York City, but what would it be like back in that small valley town in California? She had been raised with a strong sense of social justice, and her parents considered themselves social justice activists, but this just wouldn't fit their criteria.

She and Carol stayed together for four years without coming out to Mary's parents. When Mary did come out a year after she and Carol had split up, her conservative brother disowned her and her parents couldn't talk about it, but her mom's Christian faith did enable her to continue to love her beautiful daughter. And one of her aunts really came through, holding everyone's pain and holding the family together. They just didn't talk about Mary's "lifestyle."

Almost as hard for Mary's mom as accepting Mary's sexuality was accepting her decision to become a baker! How on earth could the daughter she had hoped would be a doctor or lawyer, married with kids, be a *lesbian baker!* Fortunately, though she loved her parents dearly, Mary did not let her family's expectations and disappointments keep her in a rigid box. These were her choices, and she allowed herself to change her mind.

Years later Mary hurt her back and had to change again. This time it was a bit easier. She got training as a holistic body worker, and with her new tools she can now take better care of herself and of others.

When I asked her what tools she used to keep centered, she had no hesitation and said, "Meditation." In the mid-1970s she had read a book about meditation and had immediately signed up for a ten-day retreat. And she has been exploring meditation and herself ever since. She has also used her writing to help her sort things out. She started keeping journals when she was in second grade and still keeps them to this day.

Mary's brother has even had a change of heart, and they have become close again. This time it was *his* ability to change his mind—and her open heart—that was a gift to them both.

But how many of us stay stuck in jobs that give us no satisfaction or marriages that are joyless, all because we refuse to change our minds? Maria had entered the convent right after high school. This was what she had planned for from the time she was a small child. She lived and thrived in the community she had chosen, doing whatever work was placed in front of her. After many years and positions she was given the job of counseling novices as they entered the convent, and the job frequently took her away from the convent. Her health had been giving her problems at the time; these problems would disappear whenever she was away and return as soon as she got back.

She loved her job, but with her health in decline and physicians unable to put a finger on the problem, and after much thought and prayer, she made the decision to take a year's leave of absence from her community. She would live on her own and explore her health, her commitment to her community, and what she would do next. She fully intended to remain a nun. She had the full support of her community, a spiritual advisor, and her family as she allowed herself to reflect and discern what the Divine had in store for her.

Not long after leaving the convent, she found a doctor who discovered the root cause of her physical problems, an allergy to mold. She continued her studies in the area of healing and worked with her spiritual advisor on the path she was pursuing, and after thirty years as a nun, she decided she had to leave the community and live a life independent from what she had known her entire adult life. Yes, it took courage; yes, she continues to teach; yes, she continues to do the work of the Divine; yes, she continues to work with her doctors and her spiritual advisor and is comfortable with her life, one she never dreamed she would lead.

Changing our minds takes great courage. By making a new choice, we're often stepping into the unknown, sometimes even off a cliff. And I'm not necessarily talking about the *big* changes like quitting a job or leaving a marriage. I'm thinking also of how we can change *our attitude* toward the job or ask for some changes that will make the marriage more satisfying. The thing is, if we never venture outside our safety zone, we'll never know how much better it could be. When we take the leap, when we are willing to say, "I am in pain, I am vulnerable, this is not working for me," we are often surprised that people care and want to help us figure out how to change those aspects of the situation that are killing us.

The ability to change our minds requires a certain agility. We have to remember not to set our expectations in stone. We must keep our minds open to possibilities rather than gripping tight to the illusion of control, of thinking anything we do can control the outcome anyway! We don't have to know the answer or the outcome. We don't have to be right all the time. But as we practice becoming comfortable with changing our minds, we become flexible to change. We aren't so easily knocked down when things don't work out as planned. And they won't. We give ourselves the chance to explore—even to explore our fears. We open the doors to adventure. We open the door for the possibility of greater happiness. We discover our comfort in life *as it is*.

10

Create a Toolbox

We in the Western world often keep tools away from our children, to protect them. Until they're "old enough," we give them plastic replicas that never work. Usually we're too busy working to teach them how to use the real thing. But kids need good tools just as much as we do. It would behoove us to take ours off the shelf and use them. No matter how beautiful or well made, tools are only valuable if we are able to use them.

It is the same with the tools we use to get through life, the tools that allow us comfort when the going gets rough. Different people will use different tools, and that is what gives the world texture and interest, but we have to *use* the tools to discover their value.

Years ago I lived for a time with a family in Bali. I'll never forget how struck I was by the fact that very small children—four and five years old—used very sharp knives to help prepare the evening meal. Of course Grandmother and Grandfather were always sitting right there with them, teaching them how to use the knives safely. Grandparents are an integral part of Balinese culture and are very involved in the passing of wisdom to children. Thus the children learned not only to use knives and other things, but the value of being mentored, of having lessons passed on down the line.

Balian kids learn to dance the same way. The teacher is right there with the students, helping them make the movements for their sacred dance. Corrections are made not with the voice but with the body. The body becomes the tool.

Let's look at some of the tools we might need as we become comfortable with life as it is.

One of the tools from my childhood is a prayer that still pops into my mind nearly every morning when I first wake up:

Good morning, sweet Jesus, my savior
Good morning, sweet Mary, my queen.
Good morning, sweet angels, fair sentinels
of Jesus who lives here unseen.
Dear lord, I bring thee red roses
All wet with the dew of Thy grace
Every thought, every word, every action
And my heart I give for a vase.

I'm not quite sure when I first learned this prayer, sometime in grammar school, perhaps, but I remember Sister saying that we should bring everything to the Holy Family as a gift. And that made me want to be really good. After all, I couldn't very well bring the bad and naughty part of me as a gift!

After grammar school I put away the prayer for many years, fearing I had nothing to offer, that nothing I did was good enough. I'm not sure I was conscious of it at the time. I forgot the tool (the prayer) I had at my disposal. For years I floundered, moving from one thing to the next, never giving much time to anything. I went to church, but that was out of habit and fear of retribution. I was introduced to yoga, but back then I thought of it as an exercise and not a spiritual practice. Nonetheless, it was something that centered me and made me feel good.

I would get up at 5:30 a.m. to do my practice; that was the only time the house was quiet. The kids would eventually wander downstairs for breakfast and find me standing on my head in the kitchen. They still tease me about that. Although I no longer have a formal yoga practice, the poses are part of my body. I naturally place my feet on the floor and stand in Mountain pose as I wait in a grocery line or do Downward Facing Dog when my shoulders get tight. Yoga has given me an awareness of my body that helps me to take care of it as I walk through life. I notice the tight spots more quickly and can do something about them. This did not happen overnight; it has been years in the making, but yoga is definitely one of my tools.

Another tool that's been of incalculable value to me is my walks. Four days a week I walk with a group of old friends. We started about three years ago when one friend had a TIA, or transient ischemic attack, which is something like a stroke. The rest of us in our small gang decided she needed to walk—we are all a bossy lot—so we met on her front porch. No excuses, we were taking her for a walk. When we started she could only go a block and then had to return home. Now she can go miles. We have been dubbed the "walkie-talkies" because of all the talk that goes on while we walk, but all that talking is just as important to our souls as the walking is for our health. We have become a community, we support each other, we pray for each other, we laugh and cry together.

Discovering the Present Moment

From yoga I was introduced to the practice of meditation and the idea of *present moment practice*. At first I wasn't at all sure what being in the present moment really meant, but I sensed that it would be a powerful tool in my life. I went to workshops at which wise teachers talked about not dwelling in the past and not planning the future but just being present with what is, right now. Being present with whatever state of mind you happen to be in at that moment.

Practice: Present Moment Practice

Find the position most comfortable for your body, whether sitting in a chair, sitting on the floor, or lying on the floor. You want to find a relaxed position that can be maintained for twenty minutes. Keep the spine straight, head aligned, just like you are stacking bricks up in a tower. Eyes soft, just gaze at the floor or wall in front of you or, if you prefer, you can gently close your eyes. (Note: If you are tired, you might fall asleep if your eyes are closed.) Notice your breath, repeating (internally) the word *in* when you breathe in and *out* when you breathe out. Thoughts will move through your mind. Don't follow them. Just gently bring your mind back to your in breath and out breath. When you notice that your mind has wandered again, come gently back to your breath. When you notice a physical discomfort, acknowledge it and go back to your breath.

You will be distracted as you sit; notice the distraction and go back to your breath. Present moment practice is not about having a quiet mind; it is about noticing the present moment. It is amazing what you learn about yourself if you just sit still. Sometimes it is less than thrilling, but that's life, too.

I wasn't and still am not always pleased with everything I notice when I am sitting in meditation. In the early days of sobriety I thought I would erupt with all that was churning inside me. But I also realized that I couldn't change without noticing.

If you've never tried meditation, you might have some of the same funny (and false) ideas about it that a lot of people carry around. Perhaps some idealized image of a person at perfect peace sitting in full Lotus position with eyes cast down keeps you from even trying. Let all that go. Give yourself the opportunity to open your mind to the idea that present moment practice is simply a matter of being with what is, right now.

One of my meditation teachers describes present moment practice as giving us the opportunity to see and then break habitual patterns. It's about slowing down and noticing, about giving yourself some time to just breathe and be, not to fill up with a million tasks but to sit with, feeling whatever comes up. It can be an especially powerful tool for dealing with sadness. The lives many of us lead don't leave a lot of room for being present with sadness. We're encouraged, either explicitly or implicitly, to stuff away our sorrow. There's no room for it. Same with our joy, ironically enough. To just sit and savor the feeling of joy seems so forbidden.

That said, there are times in all our lives when sitting still is just not something we can do; whatever the reason, honor it.

People early in addiction recovery often tell me that when they first get sober they have to move; they have to be doing something other than just sitting watching their mindstream. If this is where you are in your life, walking meditation might be a better tool for you.

Part of becoming comfortable with life means knowing what you *can* do rather than pushing yourself to do what you think you *should* do and setting yourself up for failure.

Sharing the Wisdom

When life is most difficult and you can't stand the thought of being present with what is, even if it will help you along in recovery, it might be important to sit with a group, with a teacher. When I am sitting with a group I am able remain still for a longer period of time because I want to do it right; I am too embarrassed to get up and move. I need guidance to still myself, to allow myself to be present with the difficult things in my life.

Ironically, my early training about doing things right is helpful when it comes to staying still. From my starter kit I have this great big bead that helps me conform to group norms. It is very helpful to notice that bead at times, and it is also good that I can totally ignore it when that makes sense. Again, I have to take the time to notice what the situation requires. It is true we can teach ourselves to do things by reading books, watching videos, or trial and error, but having the right teacher can also be very valuable.

Of course, finding the right teacher is not always easy. Early on in my search for a spiritual path I was inclined to distrust my own intuition. I believed that anyone with the title "teacher" must be better than I am. He or she must have the right answer. It was so hard for me to learn that *not every teacher is right for every student.* This doesn't necessarily mean the teacher is bad. It means the teacher *was not right for me.*

Some of us need to find a spiritual director to help us walk the path. As the great spiritual teacher Thomas Merton once wrote, "Spiritual direction is, in reality, nothing more than a way of leading us to see and obey the real Director—the Holy Spirit hidden in the depths of our soul." My spiritual director is not from a particular spiritual path or religion, although we have the same spiritual roots. She is a person who helps me walk my path and see my life as prayer. She does not give me answers to right and wrong, she helps me to see all of my life with a spiritual light illuminating the way.

Finding the Right Tools

One important point to remember about tools is that there are zillions of them, and you don't have to choose just one. My friend MJ uses her garden to slow her down and get in touch with the earth. She finds that her everyday annoyances seem to get buried in the dirt as she pulls the weeds; she loves to just observe the miracles of nature all around her. Gardening is one of her "becoming comfortable" tools.

A personal coach can be an important tool as we look to become more comfortable with life as it is. Lina felt a need for a personal coach when she started back to work after her daughter was born. Having a baby made her realize that she had been coasting along, not really satisfied with life but bobbing along whichever way the tide took her. Now she wanted more direction. She wanted to give her daughter and herself more than that; she wanted to be comfortable with what she was doing so she could pass that along. Lo and behold, the Fortune 500 company she worked for was willing to invest in the coach she asked for. Sometimes it just takes having the courage to ask for what you want out of life to get the help you need.

Another useful tool is the Myers-Briggs personality inventory. The best way to learn about Myers-Briggs is through their Web site *www.discoveryourpersonality.com*, but just briefly, the test (a questionnaire) identifies four primary personality preferences in each of us. The first has to do with where you direct your energy, inward or outward; you are either an *I* for Introvert or *E* for Extrovert. The second has to do with how you process information. If you are someone who likes to deal in facts, your preference is for Sensing (and you are an *S*). If you are more comfortable with the unknown and like to generate new ideas, then you are an *N* for Intuition. The third measure has to do with how you make decisions. If you tend to use only objective logic and analysis, you are a *T* for thinking, whereas if you are guided more by your values and/or personal beliefs, then you are an *F* for Feeling. Finally, the fourth measure has to do with how you prefer to organize things. If you like things to be structured and planned, you are a *J* for Judging (not to be confused with judgmental, which is something else altogether). If you are more of a go-with-the-flow type and like to take things as they come, you are a *P* for Perceiving.

I first learned about Myers-Briggs when I was a hospital administrator. I found it extraordinarily useful in getting to know my general personality style and those of my coworkers. I used what I learned from Myers-Briggs to make the work environment more comfortable, and it spilled over to my home life as well. I encourage you to take the test. You might be amazed at what you learn about yourself.

Another, more in-depth personality tool that I have found tremendously useful is the Enneagram. This is a personality system that describes nine distinct personality types: The Reformer, The Helper,

The Achiever, The Individualist, The Investigator, The Loyalist, The Enthusiast, The Challenger, The Peacemaker. What I found so challenging at first, and ultimately so illuminating, is that Enneagram experts say that each of us is only one type. We can't be a little of this and a little of that.

You can read up on these tools alone or consider joining a group or taking a class to learn about them. I learn best in a group setting. That's why I went to AA and I belong to a gym. I did the Myers-Briggs work in a group but without professional guidance. For the Enneagram, I attended a group with a trained leader. But you might do just fine on your own and want to read up on these systems and take the tests without going to a group or expert. It's up to you.

Developing a Practice

Developing a practice to bring yourself closer to the Divine, to be present with what is, is not easy. It is simple, but it's not easy, because it means looking at all of who we are, not just the parts we like. I have an addictive personality, for example, so it is important that I watch myself carefully whenever I'm exploring a new practice to be sure I'm not obsessing. When I started running, I had to be very careful that I wasn't running in an addictive manner. I had to ask myself regularly, *Am I running myself into the ground trying to do it right? Am I running to the exclusion of everything else in my life? Am I running to avoid being present with myself?*

Do I pray so much that I ignore my children? Do I pray compulsively?

Everything around us encourages our addiction to speed. So now, once again, I invite you to try doing just one thing. Drink the hot coffee. Don't do anything else. Now, do you notice how hot it is? Do you taste the full, wonderful flavor? You can decide to make this a coffee prayer. No, I'm not kidding. Everything you do brings you closer to the Divine, and to yourself, if you are present in the moment.

Along with multitasking and instant everything has come a lot of impatience. It's as if our nervous systems have been rewired to a faster pulse. Waiting a few extra seconds for a Web page to open on our computers now feels like an eternity. But any time we start something new we have to give ourselves the time to learn and discover. We are always learning. Sometimes we take the time to master a new skill, and sometimes we just keep doing it because we enjoy the process or we know the process is beneficial in some way. It's not always explainable. But it's certainly true that we are more likely to continue practicing and applying ourselves to something we enjoy. If we start our present moment practice in an enjoyable way, we are more likely to continue the practice, and then perhaps deal with some of the more uncomfortable aspects of paying attention to the present.

Discipline and commitment are necessary components in our lives; it is the only way to move forward on the path. We can stick our toe in the water and feel the pleasure of the sensation, but we have to learn how to swim if we want to jump into the pool. Everything we do takes practice.

11

Surrender

Grant me the serenity to accept the things I cannot change,
the courage to change the things I can,
and the wisdom to know the difference.

This is my spin on the Serenity Prayer. Even after years of sobriety I still say it often. The ability to accept the things we cannot change is what I mean by the word *surrender,* and that's the quality of people who are comfortable with life that we look at in this chapter. Surrender is not about becoming passive to life or giving up. It's about being smart enough to recognize where we do and don't have the power to change things and self-loving enough not to hold on to the illusion of control over things we simply cannot control.

The coping mechanisms we often hide behind in order to retain our illusion of control can get us into trouble and make our paths more difficult to traverse. The more tightly we cling to the familiar, the higher the walls and the wider the moats of protection we build around ourselves-so nothing can come in and destroy us—the tougher we make things for ourselves. In my experience of life, it is only when we surrender to the impossible that new doors and new possibilities open.

My friend Gloria's dad suffered a stroke, went into rehabilitation, and was doing well. The only problem was the health care system was unwilling to give him the equipment he needed to take care of himself safely. The more Gloria tried to get him proper care, the more her frustration grew, and she began to revert to old control habits. She ranted and raved, cursed the doctors, the health care system, and anything else that got in her way. Her fury was like the wind of a hurricane, knocking down everything in her path. Her fury didn't help her get what she needed for her dad. Instead, people ran from her or turned her off. She was getting nowhere.

Finally Gloria realized that she wasn't getting anywhere and would have to regroup. She went to the beautiful hospital chapel and just sat for a few minutes, basking in the sunlight that was streaming in through an amazing stained glass window. As she relaxed and put her mind at rest, she decided to put herself in the place of the staff and realized that she, too, would probably run from the person she had become. She was somehow able to go directly into the eye of her personal hurricane, and from that place she found strength and calm. She was able to surrender, to give up control, and move forward to help her dad get what he needed.

Let me be clear here. Gloria did not give up her strength; she just gave up her fury and frustration. And it was then that she was able to move forward.

Despite our best intentions, of course, letting go of old habits of anger or control is damn hard work, and finding and surrendering to the calm space takes practice. Just because we are able to surrender one day it does not mean we'll be able to do it the next. We have to be awake and paying attention to each and every situation. Just like everything else we do, it's a one-day-at-a-time process. This next story illustrates that well.

Remember my friend Jo, the woman who was born in Africa but then moved to Australia, where she felt so displaced? As an adult she became a therapist. When she first began work at a healing center in New Zealand, she was the resident nonbeliever and skeptic. But while there she had the opportunity to explore all kinds of spiritual practices. She didn't know exactly where she was going or why, but she was determined to find some approach to help with the fear and loneliness that had been nearly paralyzing her since childhood. Jo's abrupt departure from Africa, which took her away from everything she knew and trusted, fueled her fear and inability to move easily from one thing to the next. She knew she needed to challenge her constraints, so when a friend invited Jo on a fire walk, she decided to give it a try.

After her very first walk, Jo found herself drawn to the practice. The process of surrendering to the heat helped her realize that there was something greater than herself taking care of her as she walked. She did not understand it, but she could see that some kind of faith in a higher power was allowing her to overcome her fear of being burned. Each time she did a fire walk, that faith deepened. Jo may not have had a name for it, but there was no doubt in her mind that a higher power came through for her as she walked those burning hot coals. The hot coals taught her that she was not in charge.

Later in her life, Jo was diagnosed with cancer. By this time her relationship to spirit had changed dramatically. Far from being the resident skeptic, she had become deeply involved in spiritual growth and felt responsible for the cancer as if it were a personal failing. She blamed herself for "allowing" cancer to take hold. And her faith was sorely tested.

She chose to pursue alternative treatments and decided she no longer had cancer. When asked how she was, she would always say, "I'm just fine, thank you." As far as she was concerned, she had put herself back in charge of her body, and she could get rid of the cancer on her own.

The atmosphere Jo worked in promoted the idea that our thinking causes illness, that we can think our way out of everything, that we are in charge. The more she blamed herself for her cancer, the more her fear grew. Life was pretty grim for Jo until a friend gave her a book of teachings of Sri Satya Sai Baba, an internationally known holy man from India. It was just a tiny little book called *Teachings of Sri Satya Sai Baba*. She immediately started reading. Sai Baba explained that we are always held by the Divine, and somehow Jo was able to hear it. The right message at the right time.

Given lots of time to think, Jo's mind drifted back to that wonderful feeling of being held by the Divine during the fire walks. She realized that the cancer was another fire walk. She couldn't think the cancer away; she needed all the help she could get. And so she surrendered to that higher power and trusted that she would get to the end of this fire walk without being badly burned.

Jo still doesn't really understand why this book got through to her the way it did. She figures it was a kind of grace. Surrendering opened her mind and her heart and allowed her to participate in both Western medical treatments and the alternative therapies she had come to know. She surrendered to all of the gifts that were available to her and knew that however things turned out, she would be okay.

It was a long, difficult journey for Jo, but today she is cancer free and she lives each day in gratitude. She considers herself a devotee of Sai Baba, although she does not participate in any formal community activities. She knows that she cannot take this journey through life alone, and she welcomes the help of spirit and honors the power of surrender.

Surprising Gratitude

For most of us there is nothing easy, especially at first, about not being in charge, or about accepting life as it is. We are blasted at every turn—on the radio, TV, magazines, billboards—with images that support the idea that we can will ourselves to be a certain way. How do we make it stop? How do we come to an understanding that we are just *not* in charge of everything?

I want you to meet my amazing young friend Rose. When she first came to a talk I was giving before a bead workshop, I looked at her and thought, *Oh God, I hope she isn't going to take the workshop.* My reaction was all about my own self-doubt. Instead of hands, Rose had two hooks. I didn't know how I would possibly teach her. How would she handle beads? I couldn't imagine it. And of course it was all about me. I wanted to be in charge.

Even though I have been teaching about surrender for years, I still continually forget that I am not responsible for the outcome of every person's beading project. I can't make it right. I do my best to foster students' creativity and to help them let go of the idea that there is any right way to do the bead work. But my reaction to Rose told me that I still couldn't fully surrender my need to have things turn out in a specific way.

Most of the time, my mind is an amazing whirlwind of thought. It is rarely quiet. With no grounding in fact or reason, I can create an entire scenario of the terrible things that are going to happen, start to finish. That day, what my whirling mind failed to recognize was that Rose knew what she was doing and what she could do. She had lived with her prosthesis from the age of eleven, and she was now a grown woman with three teenaged children. But there I was, anticipating the worst.

Rose did come to the beading workshop, and what a gift she was to us all. I was able to ask her what help she might need from me, and she was able to tell me and accept the help. Rose made a beautiful, simple strand using a holy medal her mom had give her before Rose's home and her lower arms were consumed by a fire. The holy medal was one of the few things that survived the fire. Rose wanted to honor the gifts she had been given by this event. She said she wants to remember, every day, that although we are not in control, we can choose how to respond to difficulty, and that's what makes our lives whole and beautiful.

The fire had left Rose with many scars on her face that totally disappeared each time she smiled. People like Rose are aware that every life, no matter how difficult it looks from the outside, is blessed with gifts, and that every life is also marked by pain. They are able to maintain gratitude for the gifts without glossing over the challenges.

Mr. Ali: Faith Tested to the Extreme

Let me share another wonderful story with you, this one about a family I know. I am going to call them the Alis. The Alis left Afghanistan in the late 1970s, during the Soviet invasion. They did not want to leave. They loved their home and were a typical middle-class family involved with their small children, work, extended family, their spiritual community, and Mr. Ali's childhood passion for antiquities. But life had become too dangerous under the Communist regime, and Mr. Ali was afraid of being killed.

Living under Soviet occupation, the Alis had to learn to surrender at every turn, both physically and emotionally, but they never gave up spiritually. One evening after work Mr. Ali was pulled from his home at gunpoint and held in the street with other men. Time passed, and he stood there terrified, when an official-looking car pulled up and a man Ali had known in school stepped out. This gentleman was an official in the new government. Seeing Ali, and knowing how bright and competent he was, the government official asked Ali to come work with him.

Ali could not in good conscience do this. Thinking quickly, he said "Yes," and then made up a story about his wife being ill. He explained that he had to take her to India for the proper health care. He was left unharmed.

He knew he had to get out of Afghanistan fast. He went down to the immigration office to obtain a travel visa for India, explaining his wife's illness and that no man in his tribe would ever allow a woman to travel alone. Finally he was granted the visa with the promise that he would return in ten days to work for the new government. Tears filled his eyes as he told me about the night he packed his battered old van with his wife and four small children, one just a month old.

Of course he could tell no one of his plan for fear of being found out and killed. The night before he left, he did tell his father but not his mother. He knew that her tears would give them away.

Early the next morning, before dawn, they drove through the mountains in the snow to an uncle in Pakistan and hid for several days until they feared suspicious neighbors would turn them in. Mrs. Ali was overcome with grief at having left family behind and begged and pleaded with her husband to go back and get them. Because family and community hold such a powerful place in this amazing Muslim culture, he knew he could not abandon those left behind.

Plans were made in secret. The children remained safely with family on the other side of the border, but Mr. and Mrs. Ali snuck back to their home city, staying hidden from the authorities. They gathered brothers, one male cousin, and uncles, who were sent out in ones and twos to sneak across the border. Ali and his wife then led thirty-nine women and children through the mountains on foot to safety. He had made plans for a childhood friend to meet him and take them across the border, but when they reached the designated meeting place his friend was nowhere to be seen. They were all exhausted, and Ali was sure they would be caught and shot.

They all sat in silent prayer, not knowing what would come next. Ali knew he was not in control. He knew he had done everything possible to bring his family to safety, but now he just had to wait and have faith.

Finally, a man approached them and tentatively asked, "Are you Ali?"

When Ali shook his head "Yes," the man said, "I am your friend Joseph's brother." He led the exhausted group down an alley to a waiting truck, got them all in, and took them secretly across the border. As Ali says, this man was the closest thing possible to a real angel. He knew how close they were to the end. Had they been discovered, they would almost certainly have been shot or jailed.

Now they were all safely in Pakistan but without passports. Ali knew he would have to get everyone false papers or they'd never get to India. He found a source for illegal passports and visas, but they did not have the official stamp. Asking around, it seemed no one had one, so once again Ali had to use his ingenuity. After carefully studying his legal visa stamp, he carved a likeness of it onto a potato! Then he obtained ink and went about stamping each passport. Now his group would be able to cross into India and safety. He never even told the others what he had done. He was afraid that someone would slip if they knew. They all thought they had legal passports.

In order to avoid suspicion, they crossed the border in small groups, but this meant that Ali had to go back and forth three times. Amazingly, it worked, and the whole group arrived safely in New Delhi. They were free—but without a country.

In those days it took years to get clearance papers move to a country of choice. In the meantime, they had to earn money, and fortunately Ali had brought some of his beloved ancient beads with him. He took them to a bead dealer, and this was the beginning of his new life. Ali became a trader of beads, rugs, and antiquities, his passion for and understanding of antiquities becoming his means of support.

Ali's great love for the antiquities and his great knowledge of them put him in good stead with everyone he met and dealt with. It still does. I met him when I bought some of his beads at a trade show in Tucson.

While working in India, waiting for emigration papers, he met others in the trade and made fast friends. It took several years, but he finally was able to come to the United States. New York was his destination because that is where he had family. He packed up the rugs and beads he had acquired and left India for New York, found an apartment, and the family got him a job in a fast food restaurant. Though he was grateful for the help, he couldn't stand the work. But he stayed for a while because it paid the rent.

One Saturday afternoon the family went to the park, and when they returned the door to their apartment was open and all their things were gone, except for three large rugs. Once again they had nothing. Ali knew he could not continue in the fast food business even though his family was starting to buy franchises. He knew he had to do something else. He remembered an old friend who had relocated to California. Ali gave him a call and told him what was going on, and the man immediately said, "You belong in California. I will send you a ticket." Another angel had appeared.

Fortunately Ali had his wife's support. She said, "Go, I will stay with the family." He packed up the three rugs he had and headed west. His friend brought him to the Marin Flea Market, and that was the beginning. Ali made enough money from the rugs to bring his family to California, and they found an apartment, which was no easy feat given that they had no credit rating. This time the angel was a man originally from Fiji who knew what it was like to be an immigrant. He took the gamble and rented an apartment to Ali and his family.

Ali then asked his friend for a loan to go back to India and purchase rugs. These rugs were really popular at the time, and Ali knew that some more rugs could get him started in business. The trip was made. When the rugs arrived, they were put in storage until it was time for the market. Life was good. Early on Saturday morning they went to the storage container to get the rugs, and every rug was gone.

Ali was beside himself with grief and despair. At first he lashed out and accused his friend; after all, the friend was the only one who knew the rugs were there. But Ali's friend just sat there stunned. Ali wept openly, apologized, and went home crushed.

He had only $20 in his pocket and a family to feed, rent to pay, and the debt from his friend. His wife said to him, "God is good. He will take care of us."

They started gathering discarded newspaper and boxes, selling them at the recycling center. It put some food on the table but it was not enough. Ali went to the welfare department and asked if they could help. He was a proud man, used to being able to take care of his family, and asking for help was excruciatingly hard. But he had to do it. He was told where his family could get free food and advised that if he would sign up for a class on how to find a job he could get a small stipend. He did it, to keep his family safe, but just like the fast food business he hated the class. He went back to the office and asked them to help him find a job. Now comes the next angel.

Ali found a job in the jewelry business, and almost immediately Joseph, his boss, realized that Ali had a great deal of knowledge about old stones and antiquities. A mutual respect grew between these two men. Joseph's family, however, was not happy about having a "foreigner" in the store, and tensions grew.

Joseph had inherited a basement full of things from his grandfather, things that had been in the family for years. He asked Ali if he would go through these things, separate them, and bring him the things of value. This was like letting a kid loose in a candy store. Ali was in seventh heaven. Each day he would bring his finds up to Joseph, but he could feel the tension rising in the family, and he knew he could not stay. He and Joseph parted as friends.

Once again Ali had to surrender to the situation, not knowing what would come next, only that what he had done was right. He continued to have faith.

Soon after leaving Joseph's, Ali received a phone call from the San Francisco police, asking him if he could identify the rugs that had been stolen from him. Because he chose the rugs carefully and loved each one, he knew he could. He went to the police warehouse. He identified each one—they were all there—and just like that he was back in business.

From that day to this, Ali and his family continue to meet up with angels, and they welcome each one. The first time I saw Ali and his wife after the United States sent troops to Afghanistan in 2002, we cried together. We cried for the people being killed, we cried in joy, we cried that perhaps now his country would be free and he could go home again.

He has gone back, but what he has found is that northern California is now home. We talk of the day that things will be safe enough that I will be able to go and visit this beautiful country with him and his family, go to the ancient villages and see where he gained his love and first knowledge of antiquities.

Ali and his wife Musa have taught me so much about surrender, about not giving up, about just being with what is and having faith. My God, if they could survive all the obstacles put in their path, surely I can, too.

Keeping Our Tools Sharp

I have also discovered that the tools we use to keep us grounded on a day-to-day basis come in very handy when the need to surrender is difficult.

One day my friend Joanna got a call saying that her granddaughter had been hit by a car and was in the hospital. Joanna raced to the hospital, frantic. When she asked the emergency room receptionist for her granddaughter by name, she was told that her granddaughter was not there. Joanna thought perhaps she had come to the wrong hospital. But she called the other hospital in town and was again told, No, there was no one there by that name.

Her anxiety was rapidly rising, and she knew if she did not do something she would explode. She started the breathing meditation she had been using for years, and when she was able to breathe again she went back to the receptionist and asked again. A nurse happened to be passing by at the time and she said, "Oh, we just moved her to the fourth floor." That's why she was no longer on the computer for the emergency room! Had Joanna not surrendered it would have undoubtedly taken her a whole lot longer to get to the truth. She knows she would have alienated the entire emergency room staff and made things very difficult for herself. As she told me this story, she expressed her gratitude to her daily meditation practice, which allowed her to surrender to small, unimportant things that she could not control.

Surrender is not easy for those of us who have lived our lives thinking we are in control of the world. Yet every day we encounter opportunities for practicing surrender. If you have raised teenagers who are trying to assert their independence, for example, you know you have to surrender ("pick your battles") or go crazy. I have had tinnitus (ringing in the ears) since my late forties. Because I used to work with the hearing impaired, I understood that there was nothing I could do about the problem—not that I didn't try. So I surrendered. The tinnitus is always with me—some times are worse than others, especially if I have a fever—but I have put it in the background. I do not fret over it. I do not try to control it, it just is.

Take a look at the things in your life that drive you crazy. Can you fix them? If not, can you let them go? Make a habit of trying to surrender to the small irritations of life and build from there. The ability to surrender is one of those life muscles that will always serve you well. Small stuff, big stuff, there are so many things we can't control in this life. We may as well get used to it and not drive ourselves crazy in the process.

Practice: Letting Go

Pay attention to the little things that stress you out. The next time you feel that stress button being triggered, instead of blurting out the usual expletives, take a breath and say, out loud, "I choose to let it go" (or just "Let it go" or "Surrender"). See how you feel at the end of the day.

12

Trust That You Will Be Okay on This Path Called Life

Back when I worked as a speech pathologist, I worked primarily with old people in nursing homes. Friends would often ask, "Isn't it depressing to be around all those old people all day?" My answer was always a resounding "No!" Sure, there were sad moments, but I got to learn so much about life by being around those older folks. As I saw it, I had at my disposal literally hundreds of role models of how to age and how not to. I learned that no matter how long your life, you can be comfortable or miserable. And that, to a large extent, your degree of comfort or misery is a matter of choice.

Through my work I met many, many old people who had given up and were in the process of dying, but I also met wonderful folks of many backgrounds who had been able to find comfort in their lives *as they were at that moment*.

I wish you all had had the opportunity of knowing Helen. I met Helen when she was ninety-six years old. She was confined to a wheelchair, didn't hear well, and had a stroke that messed up her language. Let's just say her situation provided a great breeding ground for discomfort to grow. I had the good fortune of meeting Helen right after her stroke. We worked together on rebuilding her communication skills. Shortly thereafter, her insurance stopped covering her speech therapy, but she still needed some personal help and companionship. My daughter Jennifer, who was a wonderful communication aide, had an infant daughter at the time and was looking for some part-time work, so she and six-month-old Colette became personal companions to this amazing woman. What a treat.

Helen had been raised in the Christian Science tradition and offered her wisdom to Jennifer as Colette sat next to her in the bed. The two women shared a beautiful friendship for several years. Each time I passed Helen's room, I would see their interaction. They took care of each other. Jennifer had the benefit of Helen's years of wisdom and became more comfortable about being a new mom as they shared their honest feelings and stories about motherhood. Helen was able to feel that even though she was confined to bed she had something to offer. And Colette just drank in the love that surrounded her and became very comfortable around wheelchairs and hospitals. All that is now a part of *her* starter kit.

My own children also had elders as part of their starter kits. They did not have living grandparents, but through my work they had plenty of elders in their lives and were therefore given the opportunity to become comfortable with old people—the good, the bad, and the ugly. As for Helen, she did not like her disabilities, but she accepted them. She may never have known the Serenity Prayer, but I've rarely met anyone who lived it as fully.

Ditching the Search for Perfection

So many things that make us uncomfortable with life come on so gradually that we don't notice them or we think they're just how life is and we can't do anything about it. You may think of yourself as a failure because you don't wear a size four dress, because your joints ache sometimes, or you can't maintain an erection, or God knows what. But that's because you are measuring yourself against the phony ideal portrayed in advertising and the movies. Real people don't have perfect lives. But we all have choices.

If you are always comparing yourself to others, perhaps it's time to stop and think about building your own core and finding a level of comfort and acceptance with the choices you've made and the life you have. Even if you decide to change course in your life, it's important to accept all of who you are and have been. If you are bored, it might be time to look around for opportunities to become connected to a larger community. Take a class, join a hiking group, learn to play bridge. No one else is going to fix your life for you. It's up to you to become comfortable with life as it is.

Changing Your Mind

In my work as a speech pathologist, I occasionally had the opportunity to be a part of someone's decision to stop dying and start finding comfort in life as it is. A perfect example was Ellen. When I first met Ellen she was depressed and felt hopeless about life. She had suffered a major stroke and had great difficulty swallowing. It took many months and diligent practice on Ellen's part, but she eventually learned how to pay close attention to how she was eating so she did not choke, and, at my suggestion, came to enjoy thickened ice water. Ellen slowly reengaged with life in the nursing home and became a member of the acting group that put on monthly plays for the other residents. It took time, but life became comfortable for her.

Three years later Ellen finally decided she was just too tired to continue with life and made the decision to stop eating. This was not a decision she took lightly. She was no longer depressed and hopeless; now she was just eighty-nine and tired. Her doctor and family understood her decision, but Ellen asked for my help in explaining it to the staff. Of course this wasn't an easy task. The staff had all been trained to sustain life, not to let it go. The law, at least in California, requires that patients be given a certain amount of food at each meal, and help if they need it, but they cannot be forced to eat, either physically or emotionally. Ellen understood this and wanted the staff to stop trying to coerce her with statements like, "Oh, but you have to eat for me; it's too hard for me to see you refusing to eat." She just wanted them to honor her wishes. And she didn't want them to avoid her, just to love her.

As I was about to leave for a three-week vacation, I went to see her. I said, "Oh Ellen, I hope you are not here when I get back." We laughed and she whole-heartedly agreed. When I returned home, I found that Ellen had peacefully passed into her next life in her sleep. She left me a gift, a beautiful fish mobile she had made. It was about four inches long, and the note with it said, "I am sure you can make an earring or something out of this." She never lost her sense of humor.

That wonderful fish hangs on a stand in my living room. I get to see it every day and am reminded of the gift Ellen gave me. She taught me that we can become comfortable in both life and death, and we can live that comfort to the very end.

Becoming Comfortable with a Very Complicated Life

Some people take particularly challenging paths to finding the comfort in their lives. That was certainly the case for my sister Betty, who died in 2002. Betty was a very complicated and remarkable woman, and so is her daughter, who delivered the following eulogy at Betty's funeral.

How do you give a eulogy, how do you say good-bye, to Betty Conway? Many of us said good-bye several years ago, realizing that after her strokes Betty would never be the same person she had been.

But now, at the time of her death, we—at least I—have a different need. Her life has come to a close. And I want to speak about her life and to take a moment to honor that life in all its complexity.

One way to honor her is by remembering good and funny things about her: that she made us girls matching nightgowns every year for Christmas; that she made my first prom dress, and it was exactly what I wanted; that care and pride she took in the needlepoint and the dresses she made for her granddaughter Jaime when she was little; how much she loved sports and softball and scorekeeping, and what a gift that was—it still lives on in most of us. My mom passed on to me her love of reading, and everyone always laughs when they hear my incredible cab-hailing whistle and I tell them it was my mom who taught me how.

But there was another side to Mom, and I know it is weighing heavily on some of us as we are saying our final good-byes.

There was her alcoholism and what lead to it—a lifetime of incredible disappointment, anger, and bitterness that left a difficult legacy for some of us. For me, it would be impossible to talk about her life without acknowledging that part of it—because the totality made her who she was and because those things led to some of the difficult and admirable choices she made. Those choices, I finally concluded, are the most important things I can eulogize about Mom.

First, was her choice to stop drinking and join Alcoholics Anonymous. She was a proud and stubborn woman, and when she joined AA, she had to admit her failure, admit her weakness, to people—some of whom hadn't really experienced it. I can't imagine what courage and strength that must have taken.

Second, was her choice to live. After her debilitating strokes and through ten years of pretty hellish health-related ordeals, Mom kept choosing to live.

It surprised us all.

After all her talk of *no* extraordinary life-saving measures, how she didn't want to be dependent on anyone, she *lived!*

I was pretty confused about it for a long time. Why would she live? . . . Why didn't she stop eating? Why did she fight so hard?

Time went by, and certain things began to emerge.

One was, *she got nice.* And not just nice, but affectionate! Now, people could use a lot of words to describe Betty Conway, but *affectionate* would probably not have been one of them. And now, after STROKES and everything else, here was this woman who would stroke your face when you visited. Or hold your hand. And insist on giving you things. She gave everything away. Yet she was still clearly the same person. She was still stubborn. She still didn't really communicate. But she was genuinely nice and affectionate.

The second thing that emerged was, she seemed at peace. At first she was incredibly frustrated, but then she found this very peaceful, very in-the-moment way of being that was a gift to her and a gift to those caring for her.

As time went by, I began to realize that this affectionate and peaceful person was also a part of who my mother was.

That was one of the greatest gifts my mother could have given me. She stayed alive long enough to give me the time to understand her differently, to see her differently—to accept that in addition to her anger was a caring and loving person. And it allowed me to heal.

I don't think she could have known the effect of the choices she made on any of us. Thinking about it, both of her choices were to live. And though I was surprised both times, and challenged both times, there is no question she clearly made those choices.

I can't say I fully understand her choices. But I can say that I respect them, admire them, and that I was proud of them. And Mom, in your death, that is how I want to honor you. Thank you for making those choices.

You Don't Have to Wait

Of course you don't have to wait until you are old or gravely ill to become comfortable with life as it is. That's a gift you can give yourself any time. But often it does seem to take a kick in the head.

You probably wouldn't ever dream that ending up in prison would be the event that would open your eyes to the gifts of the present moment. But it can happen.

This next story will probably sound like something out of a soap opera, it has such high drama, but it is exactly what happened to a young woman and man I know. I'll call them Jim and Janet.

Jim's mother was a friend of mine, and I watched Jim grow up from the time he was about six years old. He was part of a comfortable middle-class family that was active in their local church. He was a good student. After graduating from high school he went off to college and then into the Peace Corps. After the Peace Corps, he enrolled in graduate school and got a job in a helping profession. So far so good. Somewhere along the line Jim developed a drinking problem; it wasn't bad enough to interfere with his job, but every now and then it did make him stop and think he ought to quit drinking.

While at a friend's wedding, he was introduced to a lovely young woman named Janet, who was witty, pretty, and comfortable with herself. She was in her late twenties and had already decided that unless someone really special came along she would enjoy her life as a happy single woman. The two of them hit it off and started seeing each other regularly, but about two weeks later Jim had to leave on an overseas assignment. They decided to keep in touch via e-mail. They e-mailed regularly and grew fonder and fonder of each other, but Janet started to get concerned when she noticed that drinking was a lot of what Jim wrote about. She was smart enough to know she would not be able to change him.

When they met for a romantic holiday together in Greece, the red flag started waving furiously. Janet thought he was just about the most perfect man she had ever met, except for the drinking, and she knew she deserved more. She told him that friends were all they were ever going to be.

Time went by, and the e-mailing dwindled. Around holiday time, Jim decided to fly home to see his folks. His flight was delayed about four hours and he bought a bottle to pass the time. He does remember somehow getting himself onto the plane, but the next thing he remembers is being handcuffed and taken away by police car.

He was taken to jail, arrested for battery and for trying to open the plane door as it taxied away from the gate. As soon as his family found out he was in jail, they rallied around and paid his bail. Of course they didn't think what he'd done was okay, but they still supported him. As a blackout drinker, so did I.

Jim decided to move back home. He got a job and settled down to the long, hard road to recovery. He had tried AA in the past but it never really stuck. This time he knew his life depended on it. He started going to meetings every day. He also found a therapist to help him unravel all the hidden reasons for drinking, and he got on with his life.

Meanwhile, Janet heard about Jim's arrest from friends and immediately gave him a call. She knew he'd need every supportive friend he could find. They decided to get together and then started seeing each other regularly, although she kept the red flag clearly in view. Jim had no idea what was going to happen to him. The incident that led to his arrest had happened in December 2001, and he knew that after 9/11 anyone messing with an airplane was in for it.

After twenty-two months, the court rendered its judgment. Jim was charged with a federal misdemeanor and was sent to federal prison for six months. When he told his boss what was going on, the boss gave him a six-month leave of absence. His boss knew Jim was a good guy who had messed up.

Of course Jim was terrified of going to prison. All he knew about prison life was what he had seen in the movies. He was afraid of the fights, of rape, and who knows what, but he also knew he had no choice. Once in prison, he came to know a whole different world. There were no AA meetings at the prison, but Jim knew he had the support of his family, friends, and the twelve steps. He read, he shared books with the other prisoners, he played cards, he listened to their stories, and he was grateful. Grateful for his family, for his community, and for Janet, who was his support and anchor while he served his time.

He's out now, and he and Janet are married. And he continues to feel grateful for the experience. He knows he could have gone down the tubes had this not happened to him. It took this major hit in the head to wake him up, and now he's glad to be awake. He still gets frightened from time to time, but he knows what to do to come back into balance. He can even laugh at himself and the things he thought were important. He frequently shares his story (to remind him of who he is) and he lives each day with gratitude.

Janet also learned a lot about herself during this time and is grateful for the red flag she carried and for her ability to put it down and trust in the love she feels for Jim. They are an amazing, ordinary couple who have learned to be comfortable with life as it is.

Each new day gives us a place to begin. Recognizing that there are no mistakes takes courage and time, but I hope I've convinced you that it's worth it. Learning from each event that takes place in our lives, even the ones we did not choose or were the most difficult, gives us the opportunity to develop the very tools that will bring us back to comfort.

Let your eyes be open to what is, let your heart be open. Take baby steps. Just follow the rough outlines of the path: honor where you came from; own your pain, hurt, and vulnerability; accept yourself; tell your story and allow it to change over time; laugh at yourself; connect to community; take good care of yourself; get back up after things fall apart; be willing to change your mind; create a toolbox; surrender. Have patience, practice, stay willing, and show yourself some compassion when you stumble, and you *will* become comfortable on this path called life.

A Place to Begin

The following is a listing of some of the places I began to find comfort in my life. It is by no means a definitive resource directory. It is just a place to begin.

If you are struggling with an addiction and would like to connect with Alcoholics Anonymous or any of its affiliate Twelve Step programs (Overeaters Anonymous, Gamblers Anonymous, etc.), you can find them online at *www.alcoholics-anonymous.org*. You can also look them up in your local phone book. Nearly every city and town in America has regular AA meetings.

To find free Myers-Briggs and Enneagram tests, go to *www.LibrarySupportStaff.com*

In chapter 8 I identified one man by his real name, Azim Kjamisa. You can find out more about this remarkable man and his story, or purchase his book, *Azim's Bardo: From Murder to Forgiveness,* through his Web site, *http://www.azimkhamisa.com/display/Author.asp*

Another author who has been particularly helpful to me is Rabbi Harold S. Kushner. Rabbi Kushner is best known for *When Bad Things Happen to Good People,* a book that helped me enormously, but he has written other good ones, too. You can find out more about his books at your nearest library, bookstore, or online. You might find that one of his other books is just what you need.

Brother David Steindl-Rast, Thich Nhat Hanh, May Sarton, Sue Bender, and Henri Nouwen, all of whom have books you can find in your local library or bookstore, have also been important guides on my journey.

Now it's up to you. Make your own list of helpful resources. Trust yourself. Give yourself credit for knowing how to support yourself as you continue becoming comfortable with your life as it is. Blessings on your journey.

About the Author

ELEANOR WILEY is a former speech pathologist and gerontologist who began her prayer bead practice at age fifty-eight. She teaches workshops all over the world on making prayer beads as a spiritual practice. This is her second book. You can contact Eleanor through her website, *www.prayerbdzs.com*, or by emailing *eleanor@prayerbdzs.com*.